Aline Delatte

Urban Development on a Participatory Democracy Basis

How to Actively Involve Citizens as Local Experts and Partners
in Urban Governance
The Urban Renewal Program *Aktives Stadtzentrum Turmstraße*, Berlin

STÄDTEBAU – ARCHITEKTUR – GESELLSCHAFT

Herausgeber: Prof. Dr. Harald Bodenschatz, Prof. Dr. Barbara Schönig

ISSN 2191-0472

1   *Juliane Lorenz*
    More Urban to Suburbia
    Städtebauliche Strategien zur Bekämpfung von *Sprawl*
    in der Metropolenregion Toronto
    ISBN 978-3-8382-0141-2

2   *Clara Franziska Maria Weber*
    Unité d'habitation Typ Berlin
    Anspruch und Wirklichkeit einer Wohnmaschine
    ISBN 978-3-8382-0285-3

3   *Jana Richter*
    Die Wechselwirkungen zwischen Tourismus und urbanem Raum
    Funktionsprinzipien am Beispiel der räumlichen Entwicklung und der gegenwärtigen
    Ausprägung der Touristenmetropole Berlin
    ISBN 978-3-8382-0327-0

4   *Aline Delatte*
    Urban Development on a Participatory Democracy Basis
    How to Actively Involve Citizens as Local Experts and Partners in Urban Governance
    The Urban Renewal Program *Aktives Stadtzentrum Turmstraße*, Berlin
    ISBN 978-3-8382-0464-2

Aline Delatte

URBAN DEVELOPMENT ON A PARTICIPATORY DEMOCRACY BASIS
How to Actively Involve Citizens as
Local Experts and Partners in Urban Governance

The Urban Renewal Program *Aktives Stadtzentrum Turmstraße*, Berlin

ibidem-Verlag
Stuttgart

Bibliografische Information der Deutschen Nationalbibliothek
Die Deutsche Nationalbibliothek verzeichnet diese Publikation in der
Deutschen Nationalbibliografie; detaillierte bibliografische Daten sind im
Internet über http://dnb.d-nb.de abrufbar.

Bibliographic information published by the Deutsche Nationalbibliothek
Die Deutsche Nationalbibliothek lists this publication in the Deutsche Nationalbibliografie;
detailed bibliographic data are available in the Internet at http://dnb.d-nb.de.

∞
Gedruckt auf alterungsbeständigem, säurefreien Papier
Printed on acid-free paper

ISSN: 2191-0472

ISBN-13: 978-3-8382-0464-2

© *ibidem*-Verlag
Stuttgart 2014

Alle Rechte vorbehalten

Das Werk einschließlich aller seiner Teile ist urheberrechtlich geschützt. Jede Verwertung
außerhalb der engen Grenzen des Urheberrechtsgesetzes ist ohne Zustimmung des Verlages
unzulässig und strafbar. Dies gilt insbesondere für Vervielfältigungen,
Übersetzungen, Mikroverfilmungen und elektronische Speicherformen sowie die
Einspeicherung und Verarbeitung in elektronischen Systemen.

All rights reserved. No part of this publication may be reproduced, stored in or introduced into a retrieval
system, or transmitted, in any form, or by any means (electronical, mechanical, photocopying, recording or
otherwise) without the prior written permission of the publisher. Any person who does any unauthorized act
in relation to this publication may be liable to criminal prosecution and civil claims for damages.

Printed in Germany

Vorwort der Reihenherausgeber

Städtebau und Architektur formen jeden Schritt unseres Alltags. Sie eröffnen Spielräume, schränken sie aber auch ein. Über Städtebau und Architektur entscheiden traditionell wenige – Eigentümer, Unternehmer, Politiker, Verwaltungsleute. Sie entscheiden im Rahmen der gegebenen gesellschaftlichen Verhältnisse und nach ihren Interessen und Fähigkeiten, und das trotz demokratischer Strukturen keineswegs immer zur Zufriedenheit der Bevölkerung. Städtebau und Architektur werden heute mehr und mehr zum Gegenstand breiter gesellschaftlicher Auseinandersetzung. Dies verändert wiederum die Entscheidungsprozesse. Das ist grundsätzlich zu begrüßen. Denn gesellschaftliche Auseinandersetzungen sind notwendig – gerade angesichts der aktuellen dramatischen Herausforderungen an Städtebau und Architektur.

Wir alle wissen: Unsere Städte sind einem tief greifenden wirtschaftlichen und sozialen Wandel ausgesetzt. Die mehr oder weniger präzisen Stichworte dieses Wandels sind: Klimawandel, Energieknappheit, Globalisierung, Alterung der Gesellschaft, zunehmende soziale Ausdifferenzierung, abnehmende Ressourcen der öffentlichen Hand, partielle Schrumpfung der Städte. Zentrale Merkmale der Industriegesellschaften der Nachkriegszeit wie relativ kurze Ausbildungszeiten, klar definierte Lebensstile bestimmter Altersgruppen, stabile Arbeitsplätze, ein bestimmter Tagesrhythmus, ein bestimmter Jahresrhythmus, langfristige Partnerverhältnisse, eine feste Verortung in politische und soziale Institutionen, vergleichsweise stabile Einnahmequellen der öffentlichen Hand, niedrige Energiepreise usw. sind im Verschwinden begriffen. Doch was diese Änderungen für Architektur und Städtebau im Detail bedeuten, ist alles andere als klar. Was ist nachhaltige Architektur, nachhaltiger Städtebau? Was sollen Städtebau und Architektur für die Gesellschaft künftig leisten? Dies muss kritisch erörtert, neue Zielsetzungen müssen im offenen Diskurs erarbeitet werden, über die richtigen Mittel und Wege muss gemeinsam gerungen werden.

Der Streit um die eigene Stadt, den eigenen Stadtteil, die eigene Straße oder das eigene Haus wird oft isoliert geführt: Not In My Backyard (NIMBY), wie die US-Amerikaner treffend zu sagen pflegen. Eine solche Haltung ist wenig nachhaltig, kann aber auch auf prinzipielle Probleme aufmerksam machen. Notwendig sind vor allem Strategien, die der gesamten Stadt, der gesamten Stadt-Region, in letzter Instanz dem gesamten Planeten zugutekommen. Um diesen Streit erfolgreich führen zu können, bedarf es umfassender Kenntnisse, eines intensiven Austauschs historischer und internationaler Erfahrungen. Diese Schriftenreihe im Spannungsverhältnis von Städtebau, Architektur und Gesellschaft möchte hierzu einen Beitrag leisten.

Prof. Dr. Harald Bodenschatz
Prof. Dr. Barbara Schönig

Preface

The present study focuses on one of today's most challenging aspects of urban development – citizen participation. While this has become mandatory in most western countries over the last decades, the level on which participation is allowed and the fields it occurs in differ widely from nation to nation. This shift from 'top-down' to 'considering citizens' interests' finds its political equivalent in the shift from 'Government' to 'Governance'. Despite that, recent years have shown that the level of trust between the civil society and decision-makers is rapidly decreasing.

While this growing mistrust is visible on many levels and across multiple political fields it becomes staggeringly obvious in the field of spatial planning. Not only mega-projects, like *Stuttgart 21*, or the Elb Philharmonic in Hamburg, but more and more smaller projects incite citizens to express their anger in protest on the streets, in initiatives and petitions, on subjects ranging from a lack of participation, the massive spending of public budgets or even ecological, architectural and urban design issues. Often it is not the building or project itself which is the starting point for a growing dissatisfaction, but the way a project is realized or approved. Sometimes it is rather the kind of change in a neighborhood that the project or building represents, that are the real triggers behind such sudden protests, than the building or project itself. This can be seen in Berlin as well as in other European cities, where protests against urban development projects increasingly mirrors the protest against a growing socio-economic divide – evicting people from their familiar surroundings and networks.

The work of Aline Delatte focuses on the limitations and difficulties of public participation within urban renewal programs. By means of an in-depth analysis of the restructuring of a Berlin park and the protests which arose throughout the restructuring process, she reveals the weaknesses of mandatory participation, which features citizens as field-experts and/or elected representatives in long term programs. Based on broad research of the theories of citizen participation and the way urban renewal programs are set, her findings not only reveal limits but also highlight possible alternatives at certain points in the process. In her case study on Berlin she defines seven phases, carefully looking at the planning process, key events, communication tools used, and the influence and behavior of the stakeholders involved, as well as the opportunities and challenges particular to each. Critically reviewing the measures and actions taken by individuals, groups, and institutions and analyzing them against a broad background of theory is one of the key achievements of this work, which is much more than just a case study.

Aline Delatte manages to distinguish the limitations of an intended long term participation, which is designed to foster consensus building within the German urban renewal program of Aktive Stadt- und Ortsteilzentren. This includes its difficulties in dealing with unexpected events, such as protest arising in a late stage of a planning process. It is often not till then or even after the materialization of a project has begun, that individuals or groups for the first time become aware of the project, and realize that the project will affect them. While mandatory participation aims at establishing a long term connection between decision-makers and civil society, the work of local representatives within these programs - such as elected citizens' leaders – is easily impacted by the amount of time and work needed and the timeframe of the programs. A change in the administrations' commitment to participation might also add risks to the intended improvement of projects through participation.

Aline Delatte's work provides a manual on current approaches towards participation within state-led renewal projects, analyzing their strengths, weaknesses, opportunities and threats. It provides an important dataset for the debate around more sustainable and innovative forms of citizens' participation, which is sorely needed.

Dipl.-Ing. Arch. Aljoscha Hofmann
Berlin, 02.07.2013

Acknowledgements

In the current global dynamic of 21st century society, citizen involvement on the local level plays and will continue to play an essential role. Involving citizens in the decision-making process is a tool to strengthen urban development in relation to citizens' needs. The elaboration of this study has been a milestone in my professional development and has contributed to build my own understanding of citizen involvement in the development of local neighborhoods. After six months of field work and a literature review, I have sharpened my perception of citizen participation in planning and decision-making processes in urban issues each and every day.

The citizens of Moabit, administration staff and urban planners involved in the renewal urban program *Aktives Stadtzentrum Turmstraße* (Moabit, Berlin) openly shared their point of view with me regarding the ongoing participative process in urban development of Moabit, allowing me to build the basis of my analysis and to identify the various aspects and challenges that come about with citizen participation. I would like to thank all the actors, citizens, planners, administrators and organizations for sharing their experiences with me.

I would like to thank Aljoscha Hofmann in particular. His competence and advice have been a tremendous support for the development of my study and research. I am particularly grateful for his trust in my ability to contribute to the theoretical debate on citizen participation. I would like also to thank Prof. Bodenschatz and Prof. Schönig for publishing my study in the series Städtebau – Architektur – Gesellschaft.

As a publication cannot be completed single-handedly, I would like to thank my friends Sarah Beaton, Isabelle Delatte and Samuel Soloman for their support in the finalization of my first publication.

When I wrote this study, I was an academic researcher motivated to understand the theoretical aspects of participation and to observe the applicability of participation in practice. Nowadays (2013), I myself am still engaged in the participative process of the development of Moabit, now as a local member of the neighborhood council.

Acronyms, Abbreviations and Translations

AG Grün	Arbeitsgruppe Grün
AZ	Aktive Zentren, Aktives Stadtzentrum
BauGB	Baugesetzbuch - *German Building Code*
BBR	Bundesamt für Bauwesen und Raumordnung - *Federal Institute for Building and Spatial Research*
BMVBS	Bundesministerium für Verkehr, Bau und Stadtentwicklung - *Federal Ministry of Transport, Building and Urban Development*
BUND	Bund für Umwelt und Naturschutz Deutschland - *German Environment and Nature Protection Agency*
BVV	Bezirksverordnungsversammlung - *Borough Assembly*
IBA	Internationale Bauaustellung - *International Building Exhibition*
INSEK	Integriertes Stadt(teil)entwicklung - *Integrated Neighborhood Development*
IRS	Leibniz Institut für Regionalentwicklung und Strukturplanung - *Leibniz Institute for Regional Development and Structural Planning*
KoSP	KoSP GmbH
KTO	Kleiner Tiergarten / Ottopark
NABU	Naturschutzbund Landesverband Berlin - *Nature Conservation Agency*
OECD	Organization for Economic Co-operation and Development
SenStadt	Senatsverwaltung für Stadtentwicklung - *Senate Department for Urban Development*
SPD	Sozialdemokratische Partei Deutschland - *Social-Democratic Political Party*
StV	Stadtteilvertretung - *Neighborhood council*
UNDP	United Nation Development Programme
VvB	Verfassung von Berlin - *Berlin Constitution*

Table of contents

Introduction 1

1 Contextualization of the study 5
1.1 Citizen participation: a global concern 5
1.2 Citizen participation in urban governance 6
1.3 The scope of the study: long-term participation on neighborhood level 8

2 Milestones of participation and changes in urban governance in Berlin 11
2.1 West Berlin: from the 1960s until the reunification 11
2.2 After the reunification 14
2.3 Berlin in the 21st century 15

3 Methodological framework 21
3.1 Methodological stages of research process 21
3.2 Transferability of the results and limitations of the case study 25

4 Theories of Citizen Participation 27
4.1 Consensus building in collaborative planning 27
4.2 Role of the citizens 29
4.3 Planning and communication 34
4.4 Citizen participation in practice 39
4.5 Theoretical overview 41

5 Aktives Stadtzentrum Turmstraße Program 43
5.1 A federal-state urban renewal program 43
5.2 Aktives Stadtzentrum Turmstraße 44
5.3 Citizen participation in Moabit 50
5.4 Institutional Setting of Aktives Stadtzentrum Turmstraße Program 53

6 Planning process of Kleiner Tiergarten / Ottopark **59**

    6.1   Contextualization 59

    6.2   Milestones of the planning 61

    6.3   The first phase – Elaboration of a landscape architecture concept 63

    6.4   The second phase - Communication between AG Grün and the planners 66

    6.5   The third phase – Official participative events 67

    6.6   The fourth phase – A quest for a consensus on the tree felling issue 73

    6.7   The fifth phase – Citizens' initiatives as leaders of the process 77

    6.8   The sixth phase – Political escalation 78

    6.9   The seventh phase – Political reversal 80

    6.10   Stakeholders and their interactions 82

7 Citizen participation as local experts **83**

    7.1   Citizen participation in the concept elaboration 84

    7.2   Enhancement of the official participative events 85

    7.3   Communication form for solving conflicts 87

    7.4   Communication tools for an efficient citizen participation 88

8 Citizen within the local governance: The Stadtteilvertretung **89**

    8.1   Learning process towards consensus building 89

    8.2   Representativeness 91

    8.3   Stadtteilvertretung: 'outsiders-insiders' within the local governance? 93

    8.4   Identification of the allies of the Statdtteilvertretung 94

    8.5   Activating citizens to participate 95

    8.6   Support for capacity building development 97

    8.7   Prerequisites and limitations of citizens' involvement in local governance ..98

9 Results of the analysis **99**

10	Conclusion	103
11	Appendixes	107
12	Table of figures	113
13	References	117

Introduction

In recent years academics, practitioners and citizens have observed a growing tension between civil society and the public sector around the world. The global social movements against the oligarchy of the current financial system highlight the citizens' discontentment with this system. This tendency is exemplified by the riots in England in August 2011, which pointed to the ill-being of citizens suffering from strong social inequalities, and also by the tensions in the urban mega-project *Stuttgart 21* in Germany, which demonstrated the mistrust between civil society and decision-makers. These examples of social mobilization are consequences of a deep gap between decision-makers and civil society.

Citizens have voiced their demand to increase the participation of civil society in the decision-making process as early as the mid-20th century. This resulted in the shift from government to governance in Western democracies in the 1960s, a tendency which highlights the growth of awareness to involve citizens in the decision-making process. Moreover, international policies were adopted globally to recognize the necessity of involving citizens in the decision-making process. Citizen participation became a crucial topic in societal debate. Despite these efforts, the gap between civil society and public authorities has been growing. This is due to citizens' mistrust and frustration regarding current decision-making processes (Gibson et al 2005). Citizens have a feeling that the 'top-down' process is strongly dominant and that administrations handle and take decisions without taking their interests into consideration (Abgeordnetenhaus Berlin 2006).

Maintaining the distinction between the process of citizen participation exercised by individuals and the new institutional forms of government involving collaboration between multisectoral actors suggested by Gaventa, the present study focuses on the role of citizens in the planning and decision-making process of neighborhood urban renewal programs (Gaventa 2004). While the issue of the role of the citizens in the development of a society is not a novel one, it needs to be revisited and re-defined in order to be adapted to the current political context and current expectations of citizens. This study aims to answer the following question:
What is the role of citizens in the framework of a neighborhood urban renewal program?

By distinguishing participation of individual citizens in a pre-defined communication strategy and participation of citizen representatives within the local urban governance, this study inquires:

> *How can communication strategy be designed for a context-oriented citizen participation process? What criteria enable or limit the involvement of citizen representatives within local governance?*

With these two central investigative questions defined, this research, thus, is structured around two pillars: (i) communication tools for citizen participation and (ii) prerequisites and limitations of citizens' involvement within local governance. The overall objectives are to understand the theoretical foundations pertaining to these forms of citizen involvement, to analyze practical implementation of these forms and to identify the challenges and the opportunities for enhancing citizen involvement. To answer these questions an in-depth case study based on fieldwork had been conducted in Berlin where, a few years after the reunification, several urban renewal programs had been implemented to revitalize socially disadvantaged neighborhoods with particular attention being given to involve citizens in the process. By analyzing the role of citizens in the institutional setting of the urban renewal program *Aktives Stadtzentrum* in Moabit, this research defines the role of citizens in the urban politics within their own neighborhood.

The study is organized in seven chapters. The first chapter provides an overview of some of the main directives regarding 'participation' and 'good governance' on the international level, European level and Berlin level. Current debates on public participation are presented in order to put the relevance of this present study into perspective.

In the second chapter, a retrospective analysis of the milestones of citizen participation in the urban politics of Berlin since the 1960s provides the key elements to understand the current context of Berlin. From the 1960s to today, a shift from 'government' to 'governance' is observed in the urban politics of Berlin. The awareness of citizen participation in urban development grew in the 1980s, driven by the changes in urban policies that had been established in the framework of the International Building Exhibition (*International Bauausstellung (IBA)*). After the reunification, the city's urban politics have been driven by the Leipzig and Aalborg charters, agreed upon at the European level, which focus on the development of neighborhoods with the participation of citizens.

The third chapter is devoted to establishing a theoretical framework for the analysis. Two types of citizen participation are identified: (i) citizens involvement within local governance, towards consensus building, and (ii) citizens participation as field-experts in 'top-down' participatory planning, using communication tools. Gaventa's work *Citizen Involvement in Neighbourhood Renewal and Local Governance* (2004) is used as a foundation for the analysis of the role of citizens within local governance. Concerning the second form of participation, Selle's contributions allow drawing a large overview of the communication tools that are currently available. However, relevant positive outcomes and threats to participation, as well as the requisites for efficient participatory planning in practice, are summarized in this chapter.

In the fourth chapter, the presentation of the urban renewal program *Aktives Stadtzentrum Turmstraße* in Moabit sets the background for understanding the planning and decision-making process for the rehabilitation of *Kleiner Tiergarten / Ottopark*, the local park. The current situation in the Moabit neighborhood is briefly presented and the actors involved in the *Aktives Stadtzentrum Turmstraße* are introduced.

In the fifth chapter, the rehabilitation project of *Kleiner Tiergarten / Ottopark* is presented as a case study. This project began in 2008 and was subdivided in two planning sections: The first planning section came to a close at the end of 2011. The analysis of the case is based on the planning process of the first section. Furthermore, a chronological critical review of the participatory planning initiated in the framework of the program is provided. From December 2009 to December 2011, seven main phases had been identified in the development of the project. These phases correspond to specific issues or events, which segmented the planning process. This critical review allows for the extraction of the key elements to support the analysis of this case study.

The sixth chapter is devoted to the analysis of citizens in the role of 'field-experts' in the 'top-down' participatory process of the *Kleiner Tiergarten / Ottopark* rehabilitation project. This chapter aims to assess the ongoing participative planning process and to identify the available areas and needs for improvement. The discourse focuses on the increase in the efficiency of the participative process by combining communication tools. Specific recommendations are suggested and linked to the theoretical framework of the second chapter as well as to the context of the *Kleiner Tiergarten / Ottopark* rehabilitation project.

In the seventh chapter, the role of the citizen representative within local governance is analyzed. Firstly, a critical review of the participatory planning process is carried out in order to identify ways to increase the efficiency of the communication strategy applied. Secondly, the representativeness and legitimacy of the citizens' representatives actively involved in the institutional setting of the *Aktives Stadtzentrum Turmstraße* Program is carefully examined. The prerequisites and limitations of citizen involvement within the local governance in the context of the Program are highlighted. Furthermore, recommendations to optimize the role of the citizens in the context of the *Aktives Stadtzentrum Turmstraße* Program are proposed.

The conclusion provides an overview of the results emerging from the cross-method analysis based on theory and empirical findings regarding the role of citizens in the framework of the *Aktives Stadtzentrum Turmstraße* Program. The study opens the discussion to the wider context of urban local governance. It outlines the complementarities between 'top-down' participatory planning on time-limited and focused issues and long-term involvement of citizens within local urban governance. The combination of the two forms of citizen participation appears to be a sustainable and appropriate form to involve citizens in the development of their neighborhoods.

1 Contextualization of the study

1.1 Citizen participation: a global concern

One can notice a growing number of conferences that deal with governance and participation issues. This illustrates the current international concern and need for understanding and tackling the new challenges with which societies are confronted. In 2005, the Organization for Economic Co-operation and Development (OECD) gathered ministers and senior officials from 27 member countries (as well as Slovenia) to discuss the role of government in the 21st century and the interaction between public administration and citizens (OECD 2005). The same year, the United Nations Public Administration Network organized the 6th *Global Forum of Reinventing the Government*, called *'Toward Participatory and Transparent Governance'* (United Nations Public Administration Programme 2005). Between 2009 and 2011, Metropolis – *World Association of Major Metropolises* – organized a commission on the topic *Integrated Urban Governance*, which contributed to the international debate (Metropolis 2011). One of the most relevant official international commitments regarding public participation is formulated in Agenda 21 signed by 172 countries in Rio de Janeiro in 1992. In the preamble of the third and last section of Agenda 21 – *Strengthening the role of major groups* – the relevance of public participation in decision-making is emphasized:

> „One of the fundamental prerequisites for the achievement of sustainable development is broad public participation in decision-making. Furthermore, in the more specific context of environment and development, the need for new forms of participation has emerged. This includes the need of individuals, groups and organizations to participate in environmental impact assessment procedures and to know about and participate in decisions, particularly those which potentially affect the communities in which they live and work." (United Nations 1992, 23.2)

By including participation as one of the pillars[1] of 'good governance', the United Nation Development Program (UNDP) confirmed the international willingness to involve civil society in the process of governance.

> "All men and women should have a voice in decision-making, either directly or through legitimate intermediate institutions that represent their interests." (UNDP 1997, p.17)

---

[1] The nine pillars of 'good governance' according to UNDP are: Participation, Role of law, Transparency, Responsiveness, Consensus Orientation, Equity, Effectiveness and Efficiency, Accountability, Strategic Vision (UNDP 1997).

Furthermore, the UNDP includes the idea of 'consensus orientation' as another pillar of 'good governance':

> "Good governance mediates differing interests to reach a broad consensus on what is in the best interests of the group and, where possible, on policies and procedures." (UNDP 1997, p.15)

These two UNDP statements show the willingness of an international organization to take a crucial turn towards a definition of 'good governance' that is oriented for citizens' interest based on a consensus building process.

During the last few decades, changes in the administrative structure vis-à-vis society have taken place in some European countries, and new development managing instruments have been designed, which has redefined the link between public administration and civil society. The structural transformation is based on a more participative democracy with the intention to enhance the efficiency of public administration and to strengthen social cohesion in the city. In 2001, the European Commission formulated in a White Paper called *European Governance* the willingness to open the decision-making process and to involve the different societal actors into European politics. The intentions have been to enhance the legitimacy and transparency of the public sector and to develop citizen oriented strategies (Hamedinger 2010).

> "The Union must renew the Community method by following a less top-down approach and complementing its policy tools more effectively with non-legislative instruments."
> (Commission of the European Communities 2001, p.4)

1.2 Citizen participation in urban governance

On the European Union level, commitments between members define common goals for coherent European urban development. Two charters are especially relevant for urban development on the city level: the Aalborg Charter of 1994 and the Leipzig Charter of 2007. The aim of the Aalborg Charter – *Charter of European Cities & Towns Towards Sustainability* - is to develop a guideline for the sustainable development of European cities in accordance with the goals and ideas committed in 1992 within Agenda 21. By signing the Aalborg Charter, cities confirmed the commitments – which the international community had already agreed upon in Rio de Janeiro – to elaborate a *Local Agenda 21* and to set an action program for sustainable urban development as agreed in Chapter 28 of Agenda 21. The states participating in the European Conference on *Sustainable Cities & Towns* in Aalborg approved the relevance of citizens' involvement for a sustainable urban development:

> "We, cities & towns pledge to meet the mandate given by Agenda 21, the key document approved at the Earth Summit in Rio de Janeiro, to work with all sectors of our communities - citizens, businesses, interest groups - when developing our Local Agenda 21 plans. We recognize the call in the European Union's Fifth Environmental Action Programme "Towards Sustainability" for the responsibility for the implementation of the programme to be shared among all sectors of the community. Therefore, we will base our work on co-operation between all actors involved. We shall ensure that all citizens and interested groups have access to information and are able to participate in local decision-making processes. We will seek opportunities for education and training for sustainability, not only for the general population, but for both elected representatives and officials in local government". (Charter of European Cities & Towns Towards Sustainability 1994, Part I.13)

By signing the Leipzig Charter in May 2007, the European state members agreed to a common integrated European urban policy. The Leipzig Charta aims to promote an urban development based on three principles: (i) to promote the quality of public space, (ii) to modernize infrastructure networks and (iii) to promote the knowledge-potential of cities by innovation and education policies – as well as to strengthen urban development in deprived urban areas to balance urban inequalities. In order to implement this strategy, the state members committed to develop an integrated urban concept on national, regional and local levels as well as to elaborate instruments to provide support to the governance structure (Leipzig Charta 2007).

In 2007, the German Federal Ministry for Transport, Building and Urban Development (*Bundesministerium für Verkehr, Bau und Stadtentwicklung* (*BMVBS*)) and the Federal Institute for Building and Spatial Research (*Bundesamt für Bauwesen und Raumordnung* (*BBR*)) expressed their willingness to construct a *National Urban Development Policy* and identified citizen involvement as a condition for the enforcement of the policy:

> "Urban Development Policy can only be successful when citizens are reached by actions, events and information and motivated to participate." (BMVBS and BBR 2007, p.21)

The *National Urban Development Policy* has been established as an initiative to support the elaboration of the policy and to provide a space for debate on the national level to develop policies in accordance with the principles approved in the Leipzig Charter. One of the action fields aims to enhance citizen involvement in urban development by *"getting citizens involved in their cities"* (Nationale

Stadtentwicklungspolitik 2008). In Berlin, the Senate Department for Urban Development (*Senatsverwaltung für Stadtentwicklung* (*SenStadt*)) addresses in several reports and guidelines the willingness to enhance the involvement of citizens in the development of the city. Moreover, it insists on the role of participation as a democratic principle in the *Handbuch Partizipation* (Guideline for Participation) published in 2011 and addressed to the public authorities of Berlin (SenStadt 2011).

1.3 The scope of the study: long-term participation on neighborhood level

Citizen participation in planning and decision-making processes in urban development had been widely debated issues in Germany during recent years. This is particularly due to the conflicting escalation of *Stuttgart 21*. The events in Stuttgart demonstrate the dissatisfaction of civil society regarding the forms of communication applied by politicians in decision-making processes (Selle 2011). They also highlight the low degree of legitimacy that current legally bound planning and decision-making processes achieve for mega-project development (Hilpert 2011). The escalation of *Stuttgart 21* is not an isolated case in urban development. The large resonance of the political, financial and societal consequences of *Stuttgart 21* contributed to focusing the debate on the ties between citizens and administrators in the governance of urban development projects on different spatial and time scales (Selle 2011).

Citizens' involvement in the urban development process can take place in diverse spatial scales: region, city, neighborhood, street or house. Additionally, citizen participation within urban governance occurs on different time scales: sporadic, short-term, issue-specific or continuous and long-term. The time scale plays a crucial role in the participation process. Indeed, as the so-called 'information paradox' highlights: citizens' interest to participate rises during the planning process, while their influence on the planning or decision-making decreases (figure 1).

Contextualization of the study

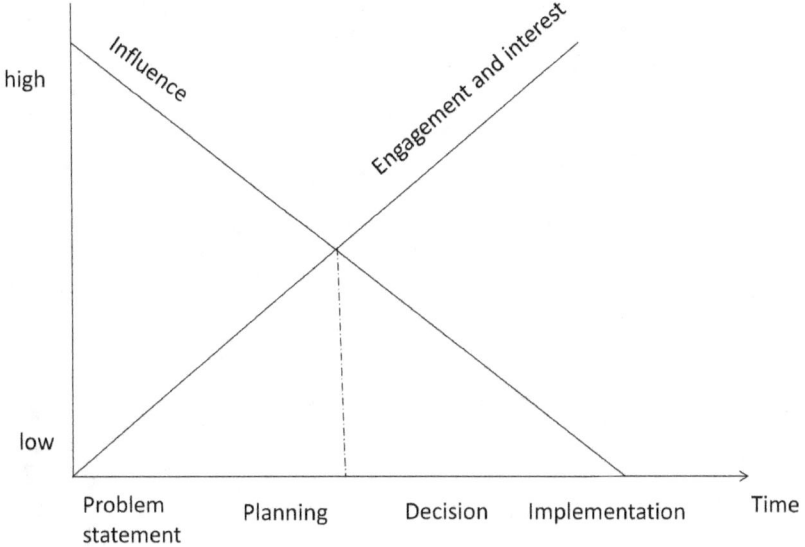

Figure 1: Information Paradox

The focus of this study is the citizen participation in the framework of the neighborhood urban renewal program *Aktives Stadtzentrum*. As a living space, the neighborhood is the spatial entity in which citizens can intervene and act to improve their living conditions, and therefore contribute to the development of a common good[2]. The European urban policy directives adopted by the Leipzig Charter and the Aalborg Charter show the relevance and willingness of public authorities to overcome the social inequalities of a city by acting on the neighborhood level and activating citizen participation. In practice, urban renewal programs are developed to achieve these goals and take place over a long-term timeframe, which allows building continuous citizen participation on the local level and contributing to the sustainability of the neighborhood development.

---

2 "The common good [...] consists primarily of having the social systems, institutions, and environments on which we all depend work in a manner that benefits all people". (Velasquez et al. 1992)

2 Milestones of participation and changes in urban governance in Berlin

In order to understand the roots of the current urban governance in Berlin, a review of the milestones of urban policies during the last 50 years is crucial. An overview of the main current political directives and strategies on the city level are relevant for the comprehension of the case study's contextualization. Three main periods have been identified: (i) the contextualization of West Berlin from the 1960s to the reunification, which highlights the citizens' demands for more democracy in urban development, (ii) the changes in the 1990s with the emergence of the private sector as estate developers, and (iii) the urban policies and changes in the 21st century. This chapter attempts to link the historical changes in urban policy strategies in Berlin with the increasing empowerment of the civil society, which led to a shift in the planning process from 'government' to 'governance'. The richness of the urban development evolution in Berlin and the citizens' engagement with their city sets the backdrop for the unique form of urban governance present in Berlin.

2.1 West Berlin: from the 1960s until the reunification

The urban development of West Berlin from the 1960s until the reunification played a relevant role in the evolution of urban governance. While the emergence of citizen movements such as the Monday Demonstration, which began in East Germany in 1989, focused international interest on the East part of Berlin, the social movements of West Berlin, initiated by the citizens since the 1960s, appear to be the catalysts for changes in urban governance in the city. For this reason, the following chapter is focused on the urban politics and planning evolution in West Berlin from the 1960s up until the reunification.

Changes in urban politics

In the early 1960s, West Berlin became an island of the Federal Republic of Germany within the German Democratic Republic. The urban policy of the 'Senate West' followed urban policy movements taking place all over Europe. It consisted of the promotion of new construction in green peripheral areas and the demolition of the existing *Gründerzeit*[3] tenements in the inner-city. Arguing on financial grounds, the Senate instituted a policy for the demolition of existing buildings in the inner-city and the construction of new buildings in the periphery. This phenomenon is known as *Kahlschlagsanierung* in German.

> "While large businesses in new building construction will be traded in the 1960s, the urban renewal remains completely in the shadow of urban sprawl." (Bodenschatz 1987, p.172)

In the 1970s, residents of the inner-city, especially in the borough of Kreuzberg, protested against the urban degradation that was occurring and the destruction of historical building. These social movements led to a turn in the urban policy of West Berlin (Bodenschatz 2010). In 1978, the Senate decided to initiate a new *IBA* in order to elaborate an urban development respecting two principles. The first is the principle of 'careful urban rehabilitation' (*behutsame Stadterneuerung*) developed by the architect Hardt-Waltherr Hämer, which included a rehabilitation of the existing social and architectural pattern of the *Gründerzeit* tenements. The second is the principle of 'critical and historical reconstruction' (*kritische Rekonstruktion des Stadtgrundrisses*) developed by Josef Paul Kleihues, which focused on reconstruction with respect to the historical urban structure of *Gründerzeit*. In the framework of the *IBA 1984/1987*, exhibitions and discussions took place, which drew politicians, urban experts and citizens together in order to define the basis of a new urban policy. Several projects in housing rehabilitation had been implemented in accordance with the 'twelve principles of careful urban rehabilitation' (*Die zwölf Grundsätze der behutsamen Stadterneuerung*) (Bodenschatz and Polinna 2010; Beratungsgesellschaft für Stadterneuerung und Modernisierung mbH [undated]).

Planning evolution

During the 1960s, the involvement of citizens was limited to information and consultation:

---

[3] The *Gründerzeit* corresponds to the development phase occurring during the industrialization in the 19th Century. "*Greater-Berlin [...] was above all constructed during and influenced by the Imperial Era (1871-1918), an unprecedented boom period*" (Bodenschatz 2010, p.13). The expansion of Berlin has been based on the Hobrecht Plan and is shaped in a ring – the so-called Wilhelmine Ring- and became "*the world's largest tenement house settlement [Mietkasernenstadt]*" (Bodenschatz 2010, p. 18).

"Who in the 1960s and at the beginning of the 1970s claimed for a democratic planning under citizen participation, would have been considered as a hopeless idealist." (Fassbinder 1997)

A change in the planning approach occurred in the beginning of the 1970s when the unilateral 'top-down' planning was perceived more and more as disconnected from citizens' needs (Lübke 2010). On the one hand, the social protests against the *Kahlschlagsanierung* highlight citizens' common willingness to participate in the planning process and to be involved in the development of their city. On the other hand, the administrative authorities realized that a participative process helps to avoid conflicts and reduce resistance from citizens. Furthermore, participation contributes to an increase in the legitimacy of the decision-making and allows for the collection of relevant field information from citizens. At the same time the then-current understanding of planning was changing – a restructuring of the planning process was undertaken to involve civil society as a key-actor. These changes opened the period of *"democratization of planning"* (Siebel 2010, p.29) and marked the entrance of citizen participation in the legal framework of planning (Siebel 2010; Häußermann et al 2008). The wave of democratization in Berlin reflected a national movement in the 1970s. In 1969, the chancellor of the German Federal Republic, Willy Brandt, expressed the state's willingness to become a stronger democracy. His October 28, 1969 speech marked the end of the era of expert exclusivity in planning (Drilling and Schnur 2009) and opened a new era for citizen participation in political and societal development.

> "We want to dare more democracy. We will reveal how we work and want to satisfy the critical need for information. We will give every citizen the opportunity to participate in reforming the state and society, and not only through hearings in the Bundestag, [...] but also through our constant contact with representative groups within the population and by offering transparency about government policies. [...] Participation and sharing responsibility in different areas of our society will be a driving force in the coming years." (Brandt 1969)

In the 1970s, the link between the state and citizens had been revised. Similarly, the hierarchical system, in which the society had been subordinated to the state to ensure the common interest, was re-considered with the emergence of civil society as an actor in a new collaborative system.

> "The raising aspirations for participation of the society combined with the problems of one-sided hierarchical law enforcement contribute to a general stronger cooperative form of state decision-finding." (Döhler 2007, p.51)

2.2 After the reunification

While the fall of the Berlin wall had altered the political map of the world, in the city the consequences of the 40 years of disconnected urban development became suddenly evident. The urban landscapes of West Berlin and East Berlin were different; thus, a common urban policy was needed. Mega-projects – such as *Postdamer Platz* and *Regierungsviertel* – were designed in order to develop the city according to the demographic forecasts for population and economic growth, which had been expected for the years following the reunification. According to Bodenschatz, the implementation of these mega-projects corresponds to the *"years of Euphoria"* (Bodenschatz 2010, p.89) between 1990 and 1995. These were followed by the years of *"disillusionment"* between 1995 and 1999, when urban experts and politicians realized that the real economic and democratic growth failed to deliver on the expected forecasts. The reunification also implied a change in the market system in Berlin, which was submitted to the neo-liberalism system rules and *"the politicians were exposed to a high pressure from the investors' side"* (Bodenschatz 2010, p.87). The role of the government decreased to the advantage of investors implying a neglect of societal common interest (Lücke 2010). The adaptation to the new political and economic system led to fundamental changes and marked the end of the state as a central ruling authority for the common good of the society (Hamedinger 2010). The change in the understanding of the state in Germany led to an 'activating' state in which the daily tasks of urban development would be allocated from that point forward to different stakeholders: public sector, private sector and civil society (Jakubowski 2007).

> "This change has been described with the notion "Governance": Unilateral state government is expanded by Governance as well as by cooperative oriented influence." (SenStadt 2011, p.38)

Moreover, the complexity of urban development implies a necessary collaboration between several actors of the city: the urban experts, the users, the private sector and the politicians (Lübke 2010). The urgent need for a common urban development strategy for the entire city and the predictions of demographic and economic growth for the years that followed the reunification were an incentive for stakeholders of urban development to gather and discuss the future development of the city. In 1991, the *Stadtforum* – literal translation 'city-forum' – was established as an informal planning instrument with the aim of reaching consensus between different stakeholders of urban development and to formulate proposals to decision-makers.

> "For the first time, the planning was not elaborated behind the doors of the Administration and presented a final product to the civil society, but the civil society was involved in the first phases of the planning in the preparation, discussion and elaboration." (Fassbinder 1997, p. 6)

The consensus finding oriented process applied in the framework of the debates in *Stadtforum* is a pioneer process towards collaborative planning. Since the 1990s, the stakeholders' involvement in the planning process has changed from an informative and consultative degree of participation to a collaborative participation in the development of concepts and the implementation of projects.

2.3 Berlin in the 21st century

The shift from 'government' to 'governance' is a long-term process with a notable learning curve. The relevant legal changes regarding citizen participation in Berlin and the restructuring of the city administration show that the city's urban policies are facing a crucial phase; practical tools need to be elaborated to achieve the establishment of a sustainable new structure of urban governance.

Current political and administrative structure in Berlin

The current administrative structure of Berlin is defined by the *Verfassung von Berlin (VvB)*, the Constitution of Berlin, which was adopted on November 23, 1995. The *VvB* is based on representative democracy with a separation of legislative, executive and judicial power. On the city level, the legislative power is exercised by the House of Representatives, which is elected for a five-year term. The three main tasks of the parliament are (i) to discuss and pass legislation for the City-State Berlin, (ii) to elect the Governing Mayor of Berlin, and (iii) to define the composition of the Berlin Senate and to control the coherence of the government's actions with the legislative directives. The Berlin Senate exercises executive power and is chaired by the Governing Mayor. As the main administration, the Senate is responsible over all city key management tasks, for the administration of police, justice and control, and other particular tasks which require the intervention of the government. The Senate is composed of eight senators, designated by the Governing Mayor. The Senator for Urban Development, at the head of the *SenStadt*, is the state entity which defines the urban development vision for Berlin (VvB 2010). On the local level, the public authority is represented by the 12 Borough Administrations of the state of Berlin. The Borough Office represents the Senate on the local level and is responsible for every other task that is not the Senate's responsibility. A Borough Assembly (*Bezirkverordnetenversammlung (BVV)*) is composed of 55 members who are elected on the same date as the House of Representatives. The Borough Office (*Bezirksamt*) is composed of the Borough Mayor – who represents the Governing Mayor of Berlin on the local level – and Borough Councilors. Responsibilities are shared between the city and the local authorities. However, the budget of the Borough Administration is under the responsibility of the Berlin Senate and is allocated annually to the boroughs (VvB 2010).

Crucial legal changes in the constitution of Berlin

Citizens of Berlin have several tools at their disposal to partake in direct democracy, and to actively engage in decision-making on the city and borough levels. The guideline *Direkte Demokratie in Berlin* is accessible online and describes the steps of the processes and the rules to follow for applying the available legal, direct democratic tools (Die Landesabstimmungsleiterin 2011). In 2006, direct democracy was enhanced by simplifying the procedure to call a referendum. The new legally-defined form of referendum was applied in 2008 in the framework of the project *Media-Spree*, in the Friedrichshain-Mitte borough. This practical example highlights the necessity to provide appropriate legal tools of direct democracy to the citizens in order for them to interact in decision-making on the borough level. This success supports civil society, which demands the strengthening of the direct democracy mechanisms on the borough level, for instance by anchoring a local right to hearing (Borstel 2010). The House of Representatives recognizes the formalization of the right to hearing on the borough level as a *"qualitative goal"* to involve citizens in the planning and decision-making process (Abgeordnetenhaus Berlin 2006, p.33).

Participation as a key issue in urban development

Nowadays, planning without participation is unthinkable. The international, European and national commitment to promote citizens' involvement in urban governance is supported on the city level by developing specific guidelines for the public. Two guidelines specific to Berlin are particularly relevant for citizen participation in local governance: *Local Agenda 21* and *Integrierte Stadt(teil)entwicklung* (Integrated Neighborhood Urban Development) (*INSEK*). While the two concepts focus on different fields, they share a common idea to strengthen participative planning. This highlights the willingness to restructure the urban governance in Berlin towards more participative governance (figure 2).

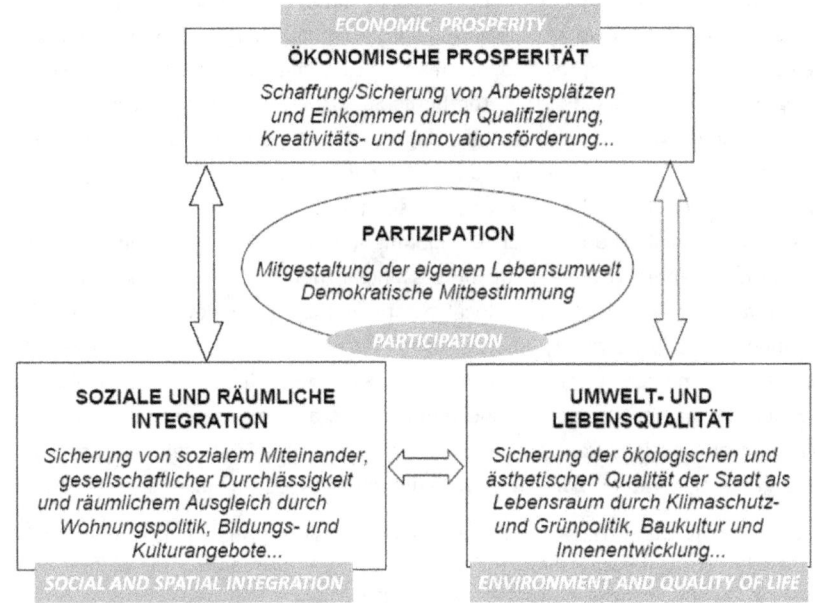

Figure 2: Framework and dimensions of sustainable urban development

In order to develop a strategy to achieve the goals defined by the Aalborg Charter (cf. chapter 1.2), the city of Berlin developed its own Local Agenda 21. Its development was initiated by citizen initiatives starting in 1997. Between 2000 and 2004 a sustainable strategy for Berlin had been developed in a participative process. *Civic Engagement and Participation* belongs to one of the seven action fields[4]. The inclusion of the different stakeholders is highlighted; although the state plays a crucial role in the sustainable development, it cannot manage all the challenges of

---

4   The seven Local Agenda 21's action-fields are : "(i) Design the social life in the city [...], (ii) Civic Engagement and Participation [...], (iii) Traffic/Mobility [...], (iv) Berlin in Brandenburg's landscape [...], (v) Energy and climate protection policy [...], (vi) Economy and work [...], (vii) Education for the future." (Abgeordnetenhaus Berlin 2006, p. 19)

the society on its own. This statement supports the idea to elaborate planning instruments in order to increase citizen commitment and citizen participation in the decision-making process. The strategy set in Local Agenda 21 recognizes and puts into perspective the social capital[5] of citizens and the active involvement of the citizen in social and political arenas (Abgeordnetenhaus Berlin 2006). By signing the Leipzig Charter (cf. chapter 1.2), German cities committed to develop their own integrated urban policy. In 2008, the Berlin Senate established the principles of an *INSEK* concept with a socio-spatial orientation and published a guideline called *Handbuch zur Sozialraumorientierung - Grundlage der integrierten Stadt(teil)entwicklung Berlin* (Guideline for a Socio-spatial Orientation – Principles of the Integrated Neighborhood Urban Development Berlin). The development of this strategy, as an innovative pilot process highlights the Senate's willingness to strengthen the engagement of local actors in the urban development of their neighborhoods. The strategy emphasizes the necessity of collaboration between the diverse stakeholders of the neighborhoods – citizens, interest groups, Borough Administration – to develop the neighborhood in a common and multidisciplinary planning and design process. The implementation of this strategy is based on a strengthening of local urban governance networks, especially to:

> "activate and use the citizens' ability and engagement as well as the potentials of the area and to strengthen the resources and potentials of the administration in its effectiveness through better coordination, cooperation and communication" (SenStadt 2009, p. 9).

In the *INSEK* concept, the Senate expresses the willingness to strengthen the collaborative work between the Senate Administration and the Borough Administration, which requires a new form of administrative communication and commitment to complete the current administrative legal framework defined by the *Verwaltungsreform-Grundsätze Gesetz (*literal translation: Administrative Reforms Principles Law*)*. The Senate emphasizes the innovative and step by step process to set a new urban governance form and foresees the use of instruments to support information exchanges and learning process by practices such as an online knowledge platform and organized workshops between involved stakeholders (SenStadt 2009).

---

[5] The notion of "social capital" is explained in the chapter 3.2 Role of the citizens.

Urban renewal programs in Berlin

To support the development of neighborhoods, several public programs have been initiated at the European, federal and state level. Under the umbrella of the concept *Future-oriented Initiative for the Neighborhood* (*Zukunftsinitiative Stadtteil*), different programs have been defined with specific objectives. *Socially Integrative City Program* (*Sozial Stadt*) aims to stabilize and develop the potentials of a neighborhood with a high focus on social integration. *City Renewal Program* (*Stadterneuerung*) was initiated to renew dense inner-city neighborhoods where buildings are in poor condition. *Urban Redevelopment (East/West) Program* (*Stadtumbau (Ost/West)*) is focused on the revitalization of the function of areas that face demographic and economic difficulties. Finally, *Neighborhood Center Program* (*Stadtteilzentren*) aims to develop citizen engagement (PSS [undated]). *AZ Program* was established in 2008 on the national and state levels to supplement the existing urban renewal programs:

> "The new Program aims to improve the attractiveness of the centers and commercial streets of Berlin for the residents and users as well as for the private investors." (SenStadt [undated])

In 2008, five new areas in Berlin, called *Aktionsraum Plus*, were selected with the objective to design strategies and actions to ensure *"equal opportunities for disadvantaged residents and to support a more efficient development of disadvantaged neighborhoods"* (SenStadt [undated-a]).

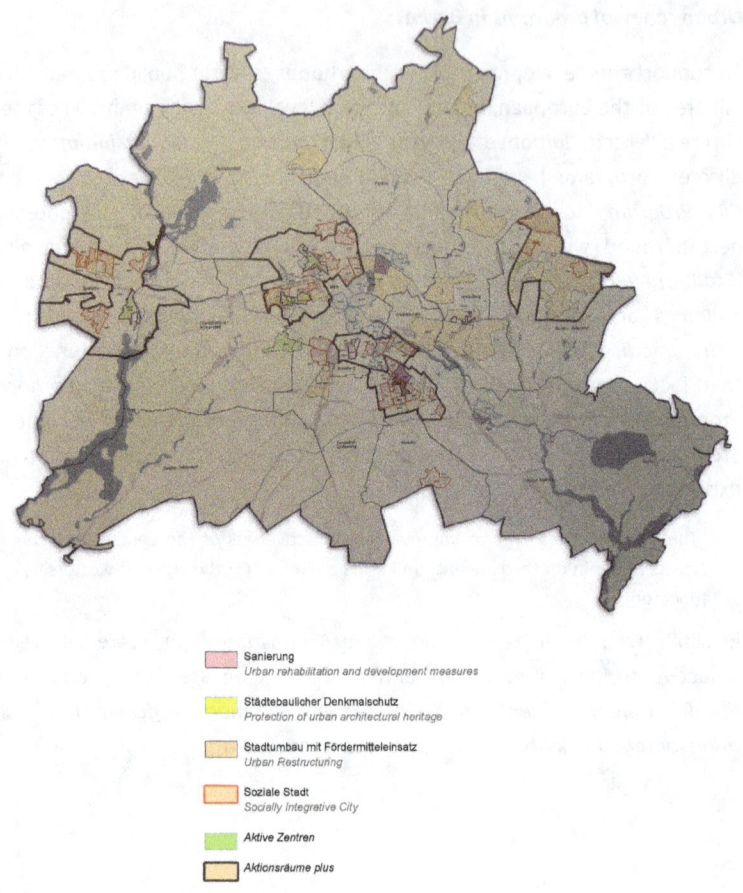

Figure 3: Urban Renewal Programs in Berlin

3 Methodological framework

3.1 Methodological stages of research process

There are three main stages in this study. The first stage aims to build a theoretical background to highlight the current debate among academic scholars regarding collaborative planning and citizen participation. The second stage consists of data collection for the chosen case study. The third stage is the analysis of the case study based on the theoretical background. The process of this study takes place over a six months period.

First stage – Theoretical background

The theoretical background of citizen participation is based on German urban scholars, as well as urban scholars from the United States of America and United Kingdom, where the issue of citizen involvement within local governance has been the subject of abundant analyses.

Second stage – Field research

The results are based on the empirical research of a practical case: The role of citizens in the planning process of *Kleiner Tiergarten / Ottopark* restructuring in Moabit, Berlin. This project is a part of the public urban renewal program *Aktives Stadtzentrum (AZ)*, in which a specific citizen participation form is applied. Three methods have been applied during the fieldwork, which was conducted between August and December 2011: (i) analysis of the written documentation related to the topic, (ii) observation of relevant meetings, sessions and events, and (iii) one-to-one interviews with key stakeholders. The interviews were conducted in a semi-structured format. These methods are complementary; the analysis of the documentation allows for the identification of key stakeholders and to keep informed about the upcoming events, sessions and meetings, while the participation in the events provides an understanding of the general context of the case study and establishes contact with the stakeholders. The principle of 'snow-ball sampling' has been used to identify the key stakeholders in the *AZ* Program and the stakeholders' network in Moabit (figure 4). Interviews were conducted with the identified key stakeholders; relevant documentations were gathered and analyzed, and issues, which had been discussed in public meetings/events, were scrutinized.

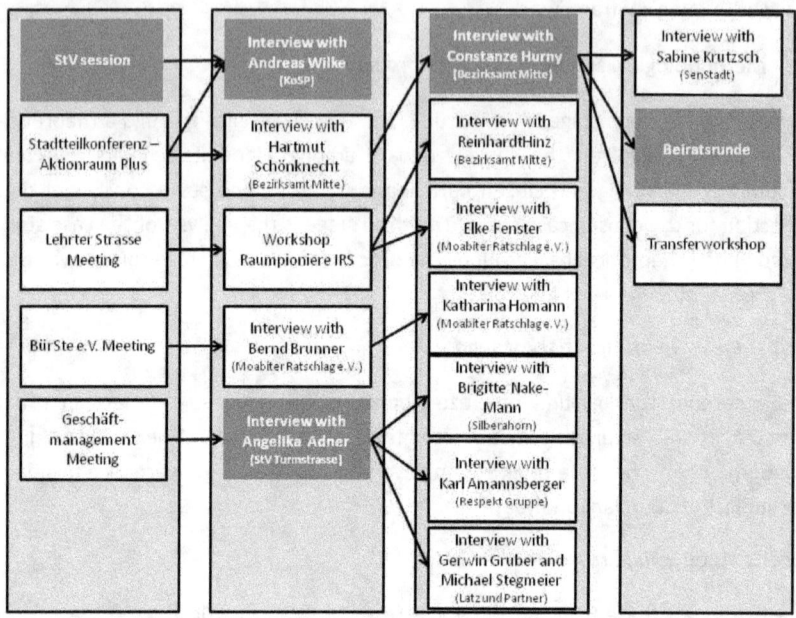

Figure 4: Field-work based on snow-ball principle

All meetings and correspondences were essential for conducting the study. Some of the interviews are of particular relevance and are cited in the text of this study. Since the data collection for the case study is mainly based on observation and interviews, the analysis is a subjective interpretation, which is strongly dependent on the earnestness of the interviews and on the reliability of the documentation (Denscombe 2007). The transcriptions of the interviews and minutes of meetings are owned by the author of this study. Figure 5 summarized the entire chronological process of the field research.

Theories of Citizen Participation 23

Date	Events
01/08/2011	Exhibition Aktive Zentren - Senatsverwaltung für Stadtentwicklung
19/08/2011	Conference 'Stadtteilkonferenz' - Aktionraum Plus
22/08/2011	Meeting Stadtteilvertretung
20/09/2011	Meeting Stadtteilplenum Moabit West
21/09/2011	Meeting QM Moabit West Info Wahl Quartiersrat
04/10/2011	Meeting Lehrter Strasse
10/10/2011	Interview Quartiersmanagement (QM) Moabit West
14/10/2011	Interview Andreas Wilke - KoSP
18/10/2011	Meeting Stadtteilplenum Moabit West
25/10/2011	Meeting BürSte e.V.
28/10/2011	Interview Lukas Born - L.I.S.T.
31/10/2011	Interview Hartmut Schönkneckt - Bezirksamt Mitte Berlin, Urban Development Department
07/11/2011	Meeting 'Geschäftsstrassemanagement' of *Aktive Zentren* (AZ) Program
08/11/2011	Interview Constanze Hurny - Bezirksamt Mitte Berlin, Urban Development Department
09/11/2011	Meeting Beiratsrunde AZ
14/11/2011	Meeting Citizen discussion on the implementation of *KTO*
14/11/2011	Interview (1st)Angelika Adner - *StV* Speacker, member of *AG Grün*
17/11/2011	Interview Bernd Brunner - Ottospiel Platz Moabiter Ratschag e.V.
17/11/2011	Interview Katharina Homann - Koordinierungsstelle Kinder- und Jugendbeteiligung Mitte im Moabiter Ratschlag e.V.
17/11/2011	Meeting *BVV* Sitzung
24/11/2011	Conference 'Neue Perspektiven für Partizipation nach Stuttgart 21' - TU Berlin
25/11/2011	Worshop 'Raumpioniere im Stadtquartier' - IRS
29/11/2011	Workshop 'Transferwerkstatt Nutzungsvielfalt in Stadt- und Ortsteilzentren' – BBSR
29/11/2011	Interview Reinhardt Hinz - Bezirksamt Mitte von Berlin, Urban Development Department
01/12/2011	Interview (2^{d}) Angelika Adner - *StV* Speacker, member of *AG Grün*
01/12/2011	Interview Elke Fenster - Moabiter Ratschlag e.V.
02/12/2011	Interview Brigitte Nake-Mann - Citizen Initiative Silberahorn
10/12/2011	Interview Karl Amannsberger - Citizen Initiative "Zusammenschluss der Bürgerinnen und Bürger für einen respektvollen Umgang mit unseren Grünflächen" (Respekt Gruppe)
11/12/2011	Correspondence Sabine Krutzsch - *SenStadt* Stadterneuerung
12/12/2011	Correspondence Gerwin Gruber and Michael Stegmeier - Latz + Partner

Figure 5: Chronological process of the field research from August to December 2011

Third stage – Analysis and Interpretation

In order to answer the research question, the analysis had been carried out in several steps. To begin with, a chronological understanding of the events that comprised the planning process between 2009 and 2011 was necessary, as well as the identification of the stakeholders in these steps in accordance to the significance of their roles. From this chronological analysis, seven phases of planning were identified highlighting the significant turning points in the planning process (cf. chapter 6.2). Based on the significant phases, two further in-depth analyses were carried out. The first focused on the 'top-down' participatory process, which was analyzed according to the communication planning theory developed in the framework of the second stage of the research (cf. chapter 7). In the second in-depth analysis, the citizen representatives of the *StV* (cf. chapter 8) were categorized as 'insider-outsider' in accordance with Gaventa's theory, also their role was critically analyzed to put into perspective the challenges encountered and opportunities identified to enhance their interaction within the local urban governance. These analytical steps helped to identify current strengthens and weaknesses of citizen participation in the framework of urban renewal programs and to formulate recommendations in order to overcome potential threats and to take advantages of opportunities that were identified (cf. chapter 9).

Overview

The overall idea of the field work is built on a stakeholder analysis modeled by Reed et al. (2009). It consists of three steps. The first is to define and understand the context of the case study. The second is to identify the stakeholders and their relations. The third and final step focuses on the analysis and the formulation of recommendations. From the selection of the case study until the elaboration of specific recommendations related to the specific subject studied, some parallels between the stakeholder analysis and the analysis conducted in the methodological framework of this study can be drawn. The main steps of the process are summarized in Figure 6.

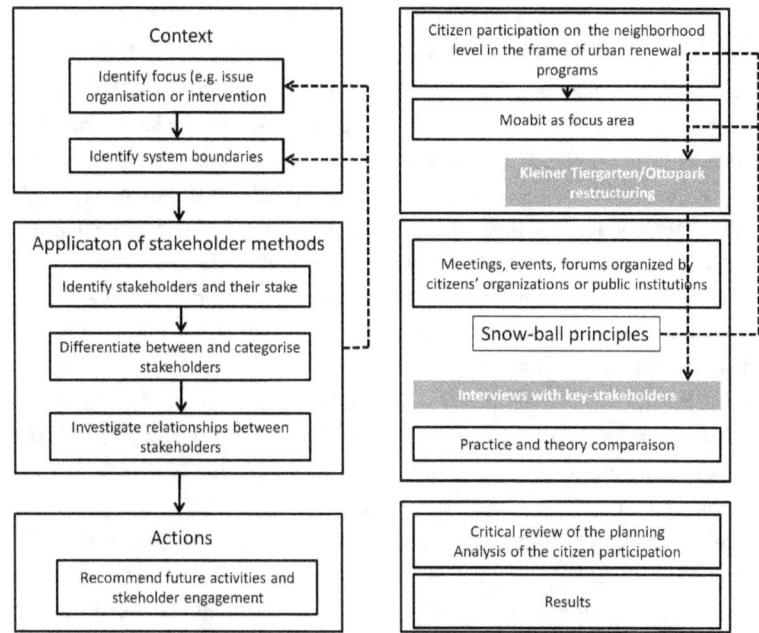

Figure 6: Parallels between the stakeholder analysis (left) and the methodological process applied in this study (right)

3.2 Transferability of the results and limitations of the case study

While the choice of studying citizen involvement in Moabit is relevant since the economic and social situation of the neighborhood of Moabit is typical to other neighborhoods of Berlin, or other European cities for that matter, a generalization of the results is not readily feasible. The reader should be aware of the three main limitations of the chosen case study.

First, the analysis of citizen participation should always be framed in its specific socio-cultural context. The results of the analysis in this study are dependent on the historical, social and political context of Moabit and on the degree of citizen engagement. Therefore, these results are not necessarily re-applicable to another context. As Hamedinger points out:

> "For the development of a participative process in space development it is certainly useful to think about the relevance of the overall conditions for the conducting of a participatory

process. These overall conditions are the political structure and process (Governance) as well as the historical culture of a place, a region or a state." (Hamedinger 2010, p.30)

Nonetheless, six other neighborhoods in Berlin are part of the federal *Aktive Stadt- und Ortsteilzentren* Program and have been selected based on a specific range of criteria defining the socio-cultural and demographic situation, as well as the economic relevance of the neighborhood (cf. chapter 5.1). Furthermore, over 300 German cities are involved in the Program and share the common objective and long-term vision defined by the Program guidelines. Based on this consideration, the results of this study appear to be relevant for other neighborhoods of the Program, which face citizen participation challenges and seek to enhance urban governance with innovative strategies as presented in this study.

Secondly, the conclusions of this study are based on the analysis of the planning process for the restructuring of the green *area Kleiner Tiergarten / Ottopark* (*KTO*), which is one specific project in the framework of the long-term *AZ* Program. Every project is unique due to its specific issues and their corresponding complexity, as well as due to the different stakeholder constellation and their interaction. For instance, the analysis of the citizens' role in the planning of the restructuring of the traffic system in *Turmstraße* would reveal a different set of problems, or highlight an issue that the analysis of the planning process of the *KTO* restructuring would not emphasize; and vice versa. Nonetheless, the results formulated in the study are indeed based on the process of a landscape architecture project, but are first of all focused on the interaction between the stakeholders of the project in order to identify the specific role of citizens in the planning and decision-making process. Therefore, this study reflects challenges and opportunities of citizen participation in the framework of urban development projects in general.

The third limitation is concerned with the stakeholder analysis. The three principal stakeholder groups in urban governance are the public sector, the private sector and civil society. The case study that was chosen takes place in the framework of a public urban renewal program: The initiative of the program, the financial funding and the decision-making are under the responsibility of the public sector. Therefore, this case study does not discuss the involvement of real estate developers in the planning process of urban development programs. Yet, the limited timeframe for the research calls for the selection of a fieldwork scope, which provides for in-depth data-collection and analysis by focusing on the inclusive relation between citizens and decision-makers. Therefore, a precise and accurate analysis can be conducted in a reasonable four-month field work timeframe.

4 Theories of Citizen Participation

The ongoing shift from 'government' to 'governance' and the several urban policy guidelines and reports issued by the Senate, as discussed in the previous chapter, support the claim that the current Berlin urban governance strategy is oriented towards collaborative planning. This chapter begins by placing the concept of consensus building into the context of collaborative planning. It proceeds by discussing the role of the citizens. The chapter concludes by introducing current forms of communication and providing a summary of the outcomes and challenges of participatory processes that have been observed by scholars.

4.1 Consensus building in collaborative planning

The principles of collaborative planning – also called communicative planning in more general urban discourse – are based on the inclusion of all stakeholders affected by an issue in the planning and decision-making process. The discourse of collaborative planning resonates in the literature on urban theory and the theory is in a continuous state of evolution driven by critical debates among urban experts. The work of Patsy Healey provides a valuable contribution to the collaborative planning theory (1997). Based on Healey's theory, Innes and Booher emphasize in their works the urgency of reshaping the way of participation is implemented to fit a more appropriate form of communication, which would include citizens in the planning and decision-making process. In the communicative planning theory, the decision-making is based on collective decision, which is reached through a participative process including all stakeholders, and thus represents the interests of all the social groups affected by the focus issue. Consensus building is commonly applied as a form of decision-making in collaborative planning. The following definition by Innes (1996) summarizes the principles, on which consensus building is based:

> "Consensus building aims to resemble the theorists' account of communicative rationality. It is a method of group deliberation that brings together for face-to-face discussions a significant range of individuals chosen because they represent those with differing stakes in a problem. Facilitators, training for participants, and carefully designed procedures are intended to ensure that the mode of discourse is one where all are heard and all concerns are taken seriously. Little is taken as given in the wide-ranging discussion. The process requires that participants have common information and that all become informed about each other's interests. When the group has explored interests and agreed in facts, they

create options, develop criteria for choice, and make the decisions on which they can all agree." (Innes 1996, p. 461)

An additional relevant issue of consensus building is the power relationship between the stakeholders. The fourth aspect of Habermas' dialogue norms emphasizes the relevance of the equality of the stakeholders in terms of power:

> „Validity and truth are ensured where the participants in a given discourse respect five key processual requirements of discourse ethics: (1) no party affected by what is being discussed should be excluded from the discourse (the requirement of generality); (2) all participants should have equal possibility to present and criticize validity claims in the process of discourse (autonomy); (3) participants must be willing and able to empathize with each other's validity claims (ideal role taking); (4) existing power differences between participants must be neutralized so that these differences have no effect on the creation of consensus (power neutrality); and (5) participants must openly explain their goals and intentions and in this connection desist from strategic action (transparency)." (Flyvbjerg cited in Sager 2002, p.368)

These five key requirements define the rights and duties of each participant and are used as a fundamental basis for a successful collaboration between several cross-sectorial, multi-layered partners towards consensus finding.

Consensus building and legitimacy

The issues of legitimacy and consensus finding are strongly related in the new urban governance structure. Legitimacy is the justification of the ideals and principles of the state in accordance with the approval of citizens. However, citizens have the right to express and defend their own interests. The question of legitimacy is in the interstitial space between the respect for citizens' wishes and the duty of the state to ensure development, which is oriented towards common good. It may sometimes work to the disadvantage of the individual interests of citizens. Hence, achieving 'societal consensus' can guarantee legitimacy (Jakubowski 2007).

Consensus building: platform for neighborhood governance

The close relationship between local administration and citizens on the communal level, which occurs due to their spatial proximity, contributes to building trust between representatives of the local administration and the citizens. Direct communication between citizens and local administration occurs on the communal level and may reduce the risks of conflict during the process (Holtkamp 2007). Holtkamp argues that the participation of citizens in the planning process is "almost only possible on the communal level" (Holtkamp 2007, p.367). This statement validates and consolidates the scope of this study, which aims to verify if citizen participation in neighborhood urban renewal contributes effectively to building and consolidating trust between citizens and public authorities.

4.2 Role of the citizens

Citizens are a part of the civil society and can be categorized as individuals with their own interests, or as representatives of groups of the civil society.

> "Participants live and act in two worlds, those of dialogue and the external partisan world. Collaborative participation can be more representative than other methods, but to ensure that it is, it may be necessary to help disadvantaged groups organize into groups and select representatives to speak for them." (Innes and Booher 2004, p.430)

The 'external partisan world' mentioned by Innes and Booher is interpreted as the entire population of citizens: the electorate of a neighborhood, children and young people, migrants who do not necessarily have voting rights (Antz 2006). As individual persons, citizens have their own interests. The 'participants in the dialogue' are the citizens, who can represent the 'external partisan world' within the local governance. They are active members who are engaged in the community. Citizens can also be a part of organized groups, such as citizens' initiatives, also known as single purpose movements, and are a proof of the healthy state of democracy:

> "Spontaneous, reactive, problem-oriented organization of participation has long existed. It is necessary. There are always problems, which cannot be solved any other way. Occasionally [...] a small rebellion is good; it is in politics as necessary as a storm in nature." (Dienel 1978, p.53)

The identification of citizens as individuals or as members of the local governance validates the question of the role of citizens formulated by Barnes et al (2008) as follows:

> "Are they there as individuals to provide their views and expertise as people who live in a community, have particular needs or interests or use specific public services or are they there to represent a wider community and to speak for and be accountable to this constituency?" (Barnes et al 2008, p.4)

Citizens as field experts

The role of individual citizens is to participate in the proposed 'top-down' participatory planning process as field experts. Within the theory of citizen participation in the development of the neighborhood, two issues need to be taken into account. The first issue is the notion of social capital, which is strongly related to the theory of social cohesion on the neighborhood level (Forrest and Kearns 2001). The 'Social Capital Continuum', defined by Uphoff, highlights the link between the social capital of an individual and the common good of the community. Four degrees are differentiated: minimum, elementary, substantial and maximum (figure 7). *"No interest in others' welfare"* and *"seek self-interest maximization at others' expense"* suggest the minimum degree of social capital; the maximum degree of social capital is characterized by the *"commitment to others' welfare cooperation, [which] is not limited to seeking one's own advantage"* (Uphoff 1999, p.224).The degree of social capital is related to the civic engagement of citizens. The rate of citizen engagement is higher in privileged neighborhoods than in marginalized neighborhoods (Siebel 2010). Citizens' involvement in the planning process allows for *"bridging social capital between different communities, increasing understanding and improving social cohesion"* (Foot 2009, p.6).

The Social Capital Continuum

Minimum social capital	Elementary social capital	Substantial social capital	Maximum social capital
No interest in others' welfare; seek self-interest maximization at others' expense	Interest primarily in own welfare; cooperation occurs only to the extent that it serves one's own advantage	Commitment to common enterprises; cooperation occurs to a greater extent when it is beneficial also others	Commitment to others' welfare; cooperation is not limited to seeking one's own advantage concern for public good

Figure 7: The social Capital Continuum

The second issue is the level of involvement of the citizens in the participative process. The *Ladder of Citizen Participation* elaborated by Arnstein (1969) is largely connected to the theory of citizen participation. In the *Handbuch Partizipation* of the Berlin Senate, a simplified ranking of the level of citizens' involvement highlights the difference between levels, such as 'be informed' and 'participate' (figure 8).

Theories of Citizen Participation 31

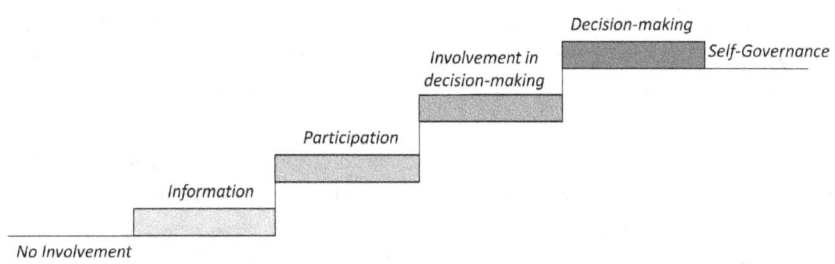

Figure 8: Level of involvement

Citizens as community representatives

The shift from 'government' to 'governance' goes to include citizens in the institutional setting of local governance and changes the role of citizens from *"'users or choosers' [...] to 'makers and shapers'"* (Gaventa 2004, p.6) of the development of policies, concepts and projects. Gaventa calls them community leaders or community representatives. The institutional setting is understood as the organization and interaction between decision-makers and stakeholders who are involved and affected by the process. Hamedinger uses the term *'Participative Governance'* to define the constellation of stakeholders in collaborative planning, which is encompassed in the question of *"how the addressee of a political program or a political instrument as well as several other interest groups could be involved in the planning and decision-making process"* (Hamedinger 2010, p.27).

A common way to involve citizens in local governance is to work with a citizens' council. The intent for building a citizens' council is to provide support to the public administrators and politicians in the planning and decision-making process through specific recommendations. In this manner, citizens are involved in the planning and decision-making process. To ensure efficient work, the members of the council have to gain legitimacy and trust from the citizens that they represent (Bischoff et al. 2005). The question of the representativeness of the citizens arises:

> "Is it elected representatives? Or is it 'community leaders' who speak for and with neighborhood associations, voluntary associations and community organizations?" (Gaventa 2004, p.12)

The establishment of community leadership is based on the reliance and trust that citizens place in the community representatives. However, the unbinding representativeness of the community leaders can be a threat; other partners can easily re-question the community leaders' legitimacy and use this argument to reject proposals from community leaders if they do not satisfy their own position.

Gaventa distinguishes two criteria to evaluate community leaders' legitimacy. The first criterion is the manner for selecting community leaders. The different forms of selection are: democratic elections, nomination, self-selection or co-option. While the first two forms usually lead to the selection of community representatives with high social capital, self-selection can lead to the selection of leaders with pre-determined opinions, and co-option to the selection of leaders who are identified by other local governance partners as the *"accessible face of community involvement"* (Taylor cited by Gaventa 2004, p.15). The forms of selection can be *"democratic, transparent and relatively representative; often they are not"* (Gaventa 2004, p.14). This brings up the issue regarding the representativeness of the 'selectioners': To ensure the legitimacy of the community representatives that are democratically elected, the voters should represent the diversity of the community's population (social, cultural, education), as well as the diversity of community's opinions . The issue of representativeness in the framework of participatory forms of governance is largely debated in the field of citizen participation. The role of citizens in local governance – in the context of a representative democracy – leads to a larger issue of the interaction between community organized entities and legally elected representatives (Gaventa 2004). The questions formulated by Marris and Rein, cited in Gaventa (2004), summarize the underlying issues that are raised by the involvement of community organizing entities in local governance:

> "How is a community to initiate its own projects and articulate its needs without challenging the authority of local government – and who then represents the community? What is a community forum worth if it has no power to command attention: and if it has such power, will it not undermine the rights of the elected government?" (Marris and Rein cited in Gaventa 2004, p.10)

Citizen participation challenges the mechanism of representative democracy. The scholars' opinions diverge on this issue: some of scholars believe that citizen participation and representative democracy are contradictory (Gittell et al. 1998; Johnson and Wilson 2000), while others see complementarities between them (Chaskin and Abunimah 1997). Gaventa concludes that *"except in most extreme views, neither the participatory nor the representative views are seen in exclusion of the other, at least conceptually"* (Gaventa 2004, p.12).

The second criterion which defines the legitimacy of community leaders is the individual skill of the community leader to interact as a partner within the local governance. The legitimacy of community leaders can also be considered in terms of their abilities to *"represent a wider constituency"* (Barnes et al. 2004, p.62). With this understanding of representativeness, community leaders are not necessarily residents of the area, though they are citizens with relative experience and an ability to represent the interest of the community in front of the local governance. One of the most challenging tasks of community leaders is to play the role of 'interpreters' between the community's citizens and others partners. They have to develop double skills: first, as 'insiders' within the local governance, which requires negotiating and bureaucratic abilities, and second, as 'outsiders', who represent the interest of the citizens. The ability of the community leaders to play the role of 'outsiders-insiders' reinforces the trust link between the local government and the citizens. Community representatives have to possess skills in accounting and negotiating bureaucracy and be available for an intensive workload, which often goes unrewarded (Gaventa 2004). Figure 9 illustrates the notion of 'outsiders-insiders' as understood in this study.

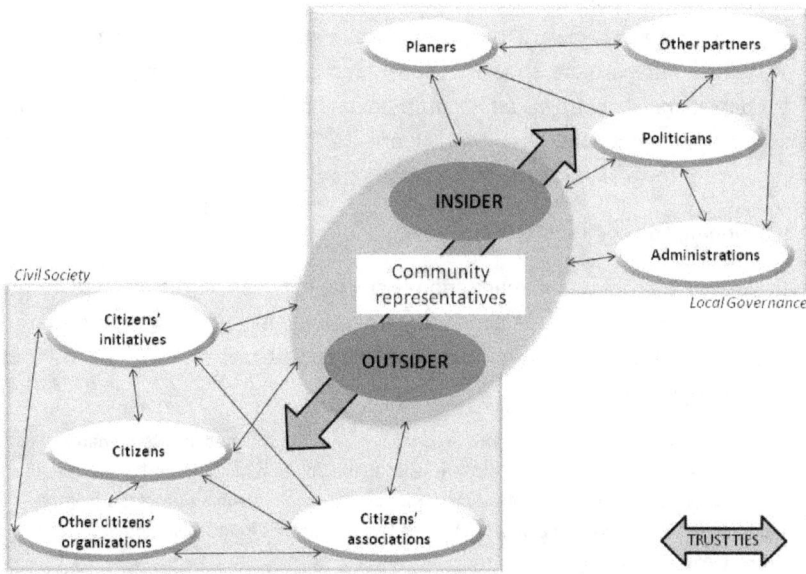

Figure 9: Community representatives as 'insiders-outsiders'

Gaventa's key lessons for an effective partnership within local governance

The key lessons learnt from international practices on *"how to build more effective participation and representation in the context of neighborhood renewal"* are presented below (Gaventa 2004, p.25):

- Ensure a right for participation by legal provisions
- Have a solid knowledge of the local social, political and administrative context and the existing partnerships
- Support the community leaders to enhance their skills as 'insiders-outsiders'
- Assist local government to shift from acting *"for the community"* to acting *"with the community"* (Gaventa 2004, p.27)
- Define clearly the role and function of the different partners and the process for decision-making process in an unanimous, committed guideline
- Encourage citizens' engagement by applying the outcomes of the decision-making committed by the partners
- Identify the existing civil society entities, network and build alliances to support the cohesion of civil society
- Challenge the existing unequal power distribution and define the new powerties between partners
- Take time and be aware that governance re-structuring is a learning process in which the partners should be open for changes *"not only in rules and procedures, but also in culture, attitudes and behaviors"* (Gaventa 2004, p.32)

These recommendations are practice-oriented and underpin the analytical framework of the analysis in the chosen case study.

4.3 Planning and communication

In the planning process, communication is crucial between all the affected groups: experts from the different fields of urban development, planning administrators, politicians, public administrators, members of the private sector, citizens and society on whole (Selle 1996).

> "Planning is communication: explore, inform, present, discuss, mediate, coordinate, gain acceptance, participate, argue a consensus, search a solution in common [and] promote action ... all these are communication tasks. [...] The whole planning process - from the definition of problems to the implementation of the solutions found – is a communication task". (Selle 1996, p.11)

Bischoff and his collaborators highlight the necessity of communication in a planning process, which allows urban experts to elaborate solutions that are appropriate to the legal context. This, in turn, allows for achieving the defined objectives, which become possible with the resources that are available.

Communication happens on each level: between the several departments of the public administration involved in the project, between politicians and the public administration, between the several urban planners involved with the private sector and with the citizens (Bischoff et al. 2005).

Formal and informal forms of participation

Within the scope of participation two spheres need to be differentiated: (i) the formal forms of participation, which are legally defined and administratively anchored, and (ii) the informal forms. The formal and informal forms are complementary in the planning process.

Several legal texts define the framework of formal participation: the *Baugesetzbuch (BauGB)* (German building code), the *Verfassung von Berlin (VvB)* (Berlin Constitution) and the *Bezirksverwaltungsgesetz* (Borough Administrative Legal Code). Citizens have a legal right to participate in the planning and decision-making process. This right is supported, in practice, by formal participation tools. The *Direct Democracy in Berlin* guideline describes the legal rules for applying direct democracy tools, which are available to citizens (cf. chapter 2.3). On the city level, by organizing a petition, citizens have the possibility to exercise their right to a hearing in front of the House of Representatives (*Volksinitiative*) and to proclaim the organization of a referendum (*Volksbegehren und Volksentscheid*). Similar to the state referendum, citizens have the right to call for a referendum on the borough level (*Bürgerbegehren und Bürgerentscheid*). On borough level, the *Bezirksverwaltunggesetz* guarantees 'resident participation' (*Mitwirkung der Einwohnerschaft*), with several tools available: 'resident information' (*Unterrichtung der Einwohnerschaft*), 'resident meeting' (*Einwohnerschaftversammlung*), 'resident question time' (*Einwohnerfragestunde*) and 'resident request' (*Einwohnerantrag*) (Die Landesabstimmungsleiterin 2011).

Informal participation tools are additional forms of participation which ensure the emphasis of citizens involvement with specific objectives. For instance, informal participation tools allow for outreach to a larger part of civil society, or to involve a target-group in a specific phase of planning. If the application of informal participation tools are not defined in a legal framework, several guidelines had been published to support planners, organizations and public authorities to implement participatory planning in an efficient way and to evaluate which form of participation is appropriate for the expected objectives (UN-HABITAT 2001, SenStadt 2011, Ley and Weitz 2003).

Communication forms according to Bischoff, Selle and Sinning

Since the rise of citizen involvement in the planning process in the 1980s, communication forms, tools and processes have been experimented with and developed. A large portion of literature is allocated to this area of study and guidelines have been developed to support the organization of participative planning (Wegweiser Bürgergesellschaft [undated], Partizipation und nachhaltige Entwicklung in Europa [undated]). Bischoff, Selle and Sinning subdivide the forms of communication in the planning processes according to their corresponding functions: to inform, to participate and to cooperate (Bischoff et al. 2005). This subdivision corresponds to the level of citizens' involvement mentioned in the *Handbuch Partizipation* of the Berlin Senate (cf. chapter 4.2). They developed criteria to sort and categorize the communication forms according to the following characteristics:
- Suitability to address issues for a target group
- Number of citizens reached / involved
- Suitability according to planning phases
- Intensity of citizen participation
- Long-term or short-term form of communication
- Degree of representativeness (middle or direct)
- Legal framework
- Design of the communication process

The classification is summarized in Appendix 1 and provides a practical guide to make an initial estimation of the appropriate forms of communication according to the project's context and the expected objectives. Selected forms of communication, which are relevant for the analysis of the case study, are explained in detail in the following paragraphs.

Citizen participation in the development of the concept:

The citizens involvement in the early phases of a project increases the citizens' motivation to participate in the phases of the planning that follow. To elicit citizens' creativity for concept formation communication tools such as 'Planning for Real',

'Local Ideas Actions' (*Aktion Ortsidee*) and 'Action Planning' (*Perspektivenwerkstatt*) are applicable.

To overcome the social barriers and reach a large part of the population, 'Planning for Real' is a suitable communication tool, which can be initiated by a group of citizens to raise inhabitants' interest in the development of their neighborhood. The initiators build a three-dimensional model of the planning area and go to strategic public spaces in the neighborhood to interact with local residents, and then complete the model by integrating the concerns and proposals of the citizens. The results are reported in a final presentation. The form of communication within 'Planning for Real' allows for social barriers, such as language, education and technical knowledge in a relaxed and non-hierarchic discussion, to be overcome:

> "The persuasive power of Planning for Real is that creative potential and social competences of the involved citizens are used." (Bischoff et al. 2005, p.136)

Local Ideas Action *(Aktion Ortsidee)* is a multi-step communication process, which aims to activate citizens' engagement and creativity in order to form a preliminary concept. This concept is intended for use by the public administration as a preliminary step for the development of detailed plans. Additionally, it involves the different interest groups concerned with the project and gives an opportunity for every citizen to participate in a transparent and public process.

Action Planning *(Perspektivenwerkstatt)* provides a process that is:

> "an intensive multi-day planning process during which a team of experts and stakeholders create a holistic growth or development plan that reflects the input of a community that is involved via a series of feedback loops." (Girling et al. 2006, p. 113)

The advantages of Action Planning are that it is both a work-intensive and a result-oriented process run in a short time. Nevertheless, the organization of Action Planning is time-consuming and requires the skills of experts before and after the multi-day planning process.

Continuous and long-term citizen participation

In order to establish a long-term framework for citizen participation communication tools such as building workgroups, organizing forums or enhancing eParticipation are the most appropriate to use. The next section shows the reasons why it is so.

A workgroup is formed by assembling a limited number of members who have the task of handling a specific issue in an ongoing process. It is usually built for a long-term, flexible process to support an ongoing urban development. Therefore, members of the workgroup meet regularly and must follow a methodological working structure – with the support of technical experts, if necessary – in order to reach the desired results. To ensure their influence in the planning and decision-making process, the results have to be transparent to the public and defended in front of the public administration and politicians. Bischoff and his collaborators insist on the relevance of defining the role of workgroups in the planning process:

> "In all cases, the potential interface to other planning and decision-making processes as well as to collaboration and feedback of decision-making entities has to be well covered at the beginning of the process to ensure the applicability of the work". (Bischoff et al. 2005, p.128)

A forum is a long-term form of communication which contributes to establishing a regular information exchange and discussion between stakeholders. The aim of the forum is to reach out to a large part of the population and to ensure a transparent information-flow, to identify conflict and solve problems. By reporting the results of the discussion to decision-makers, the proposals from citizens can have direct effect on the elaboration of concepts or projects.

eParticipation is a form of communication which can be applied to different degrees of participation: from an exchange of opinions to a voting process to an open discussion between stakeholders. Nonetheless, eParticipation is a complementary form of communication within a communication strategy and cannot be a sufficient participation tool. eParticipation provides a new space for citizen participation, though as Kubicek warns us, citizens' interest in participatory planning does not increase via eParticipation:

> "If citizens are not interested in participating in an urban planning process, they will not do so just because they could do it via the Internet". (Kubicek 2010, p.168)

Balancing divergent interests

In a conflicting situation, communication processes of mediation are recommended to avoid seeking legal recourses. Mediation can be applied in different forms with a round table being one of them.

Round tables are appropriate for consensus-oriented processes. The stakeholders who participate at the round table are representatives of diverse groups, associations, initiatives, experts or public administrations. Each stakeholder representative has the same right and duty in the process. The aim of a round table is to formulate common proposals, which are then submitted to decision-makers. Therefore, the formality of the results (bound or unbound proposals) has to be clearly defined and accepted by every stakeholder at the beginning of the process. The representatives who take part in the process should carry weight in their own groups *"in order that the committed decision will also be understood outside the round tables"* (Bischoff et al. 2005, p.186).

The advisory council (*Beiratsrunde*) is a derived form of workgroup with the task of coordinating the planning process. The members of the advisory council are usually the decision-makers and the responsible actors for the project. In such meetings the participants exchange information, initiate development and solve conflicts.

4.4 Citizen participation in practice

Through practice, relevant outcomes of participative planning gained prominence. In the evaluation of participatory planning, Kubicek and his collaborators summarize the effects and application of citizen participation in three main issues:

(i) "To find solutions for societal problems", (ii) "to enhance the inclusion and compensation of the citizens' needs and interests" and (iii) "to promote understandability and acceptance of the projects" (Kubicek et al 2011, p.10). In additional to these three aspects, Foot identifies three objectives of citizens' involvement in governance:

> "(i) to improve the design and responsiveness of services and thereby improve outcomes such as social inclusion, equality, and service satisfaction; (ii) to create links between communities and providers, and between different communities; this builds social capital and improves social cohesion, i.e. it improves networks, understanding and co-operation and (iii) to improve the quality of decision-making and the legitimacy and accountability of local governance institutions and partnerships; this builds trust in democratic institutions and encourages civic participation." (Foot 2009, p.4)

Although a systematic evaluation scheme to measure the efficiency of citizen participation has yet to be developed in planning or in other fields of social study (Kubicek et al. 2011), the abundant and diverse participation forms applied in practice show that participation and citizens' involvement in local governance had failed due to the following aspects:
- Fear on the part of public authorities related to the loss of power that is accompanied by sharing it among partners within the local governance
- Different 'languages' amongst the stakeholders and technical constraints which are often difficult to overcome
- Difficulty in discussing technical decisions which are presented in the terminology of experts – *"citizen orientation means often additional workloading and risks"* (Hüttinger and Selle 2008, p.164)
- Weakness of long-term citizen participation due to time limitations of subsidized programs and to structural changes of the stakeholders (administrative, political, social changes, etc.) (Hüttinger and Selle 2008).

The scope of a collaborative process in which citizens are involved should clearly define the action area and degree of involvement of each stakeholder in the decision-making process. Without a defined explanation of the role of the different actors in the achievement of the goal, the process could lead to frustration and to the discouragement of stakeholders' engagement. In monitoring the collaborative process applied to the development of the Berlin *Local Agenda 21*, Baumann identified qualitative criteria which guide the collaborative process. These are:
- Implementing a result-oriented process
- Maintaining flexibility in the design of process
- Ensuring a representative participation by involving minority groups
- Establishing a precise definition of the goal within the collaborative process
- Defining the legal value and liability of the results at the beginning
- Managing the time for the process with milestones and a clear time schedule for the participants
- Explaining the use of the results at the beginning in order to identify the next steps
- Assigning responsibilities to the diverse actors involved
- Estimating a transparent financial plan
- Presenting an existing budget to ensure the implementation of the expected goals

- Monitoring the process continuously so as to correct the process as it is in progress
- Implementing some mid-term measures to motivate participants to continue
- Implementing or applying the project or concept as soon as possible after the process to link the action to the reflection (Baumann 2002)

4.5 Theoretical overview

As a form of decision-making, consensus building appears to be an appropriate way to strengthen the trust relationship between civil society and local public authorities. The principles of consensus building are transparent communication and an equal sharing of power between stakeholders. The role of the citizen in consensus building is described by Gaventa as an 'outsider-insider' community representative. This theoretical review highlights the relevance of the context-oriented definition of representativeness of community leaders, the high degree of skills that the role of 'outsider-insider' requires and the re-shaping of the current mechanism of representative democracy that community leaders' involvement entails. In the process of participatory planning, citizens are identified as field-experts with different degrees of social capital. Activating citizens at an early phase of a project contributes to strengthening the community's cohesion and to developing the common good. In practice, several communication tools have been elaborated to apply participatory processes, which have to be carried out in a context-oriented approach in order to overcome the current threats of participation, such as technical and social 'linguistic' barriers. Two threats of participation resulting from empirically-driven theory are especially relevant in the framework of participation within the institutional setting of urban renewal program: (i) the fear of losing power on part of the public authorities, and (ii) the sustainability of community leaders' involvement beyond urban renewal program.

5 Aktives Stadtzentrum Turmstraße Program

5.1 A federal-state urban renewal program

Aktive Stadt- und Ortsteilzentren is an urban development program initiated in 2008 and financed by the German Federal Government and the federal states. The overall aim of the program is to support the development of centers and sub-centers of German cities by implementing *"measures to regenerate and develop central supply areas suffering from functional and structural decline"* (BMVBS 2011, p.13). As a heterogeneous polycentric city-state, Berlin takes part in the program. On the one hand, some centers of Berlin are economically and socially well-developed offering a broad diversity of services for their residents and those with regional and international interests. Whereas these centers belong to the most developed areas of Berlin, the current global competitiveness – which drives the urban development of cities – continuously challenges the capability of these centers to adapt to the increasing exigencies required to maintain Berlin's status as a global city. On the other hand, several centers in Berlin suffer deep social and economic problems. Six of Berlin's centers[6] have been selected to be a part of *Aktive Stadt- und Ortsteilzentren* Program (figure 10) (SenStadt 2008). The selection of the program areas is based on the analysis and evaluation of the development concept elaborated by the Borough Administrations of Berlin, and furthermore the selection is based on the degree of social problems that the focus areas face (BMVBS 2011).

---

[6] Müllerstraße, Karl-Marx-Straße, Turmstraße, Marzahn Promenade, City West, Wilhelmstraße.

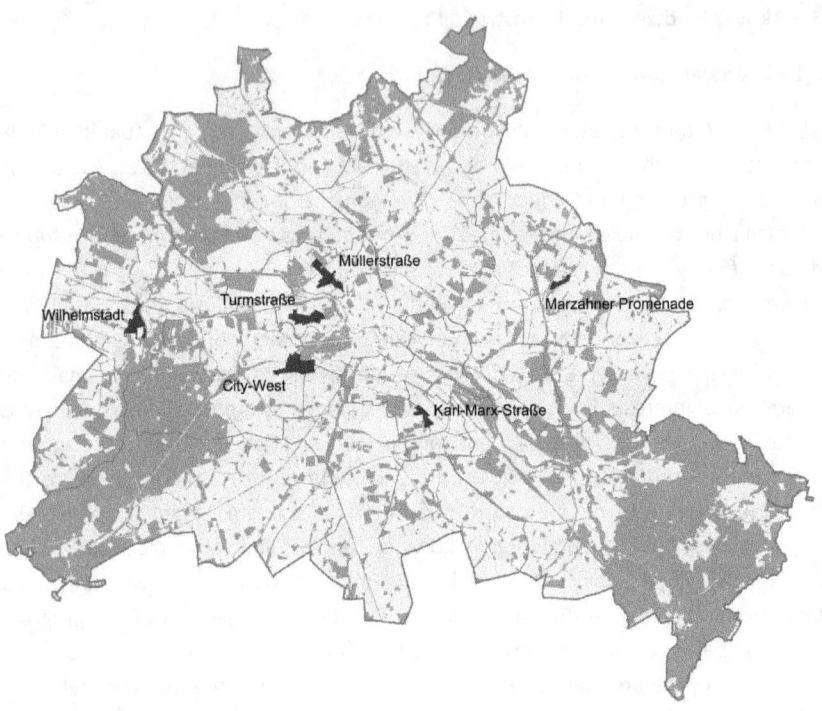

Figure 10: *Aktive Zentren* in Berlin

5.2 Aktives Stadtzentrum Turmstraße

Turmstraße is a traditional commercial street in the core of *Stadtteil* Moabit. In 2008, Turmstraße was selected for the *Aktive Stadt- und Ortsteilzentren* Program, or *Aktive Zentren* (*AZ*) Program as it is called in Berlin. The literal translation of the German notion *Stadtteil* is 'a part of the city'. The Spree River and its canals physically delimitate the *Stadtteil* Moabit as an 'island' in the historical inner-city of Berlin. The definition of neighborhood as *"a delineated area within physical boundaries where people identify their home and where they live out and organize their private lives"* (Power 2004, p.2) supports the identification of Moabit as a neighborhood of Berlin, located in the administrative borough Mitte.

Figure 11: Moabit, neighborhood of the borough Berlin-Mitte

Due to its central location in Berlin, Moabit is well connected to the rest of the city by the public transportation network, as well as by the transportation axes which run from North to South along Beusselstraße and Stromstraße, and East to West along Turmstraße and Alt-Moabit (figure 12). At the same time, several modernized and attractive areas surround Moabit: the City West neighborhood, the Berlin University of Technology campus (TU Berlin), the Government Area (*Regierungsviertel*) and the Heidestraße area, which is currently in development (figure 13) (SenStadt 2010). The proximity of attractive areas can be interpreted as an opportunity for Moabit, or it can be seen as a threat to the stability of the current social structure. On the one hand, the urban development of Moabit will lead to an increase in the attractiveness of the neighborhood for new potential residents and will support the economic development. On the other hand, it could accelerate the gentrification process in Moabit, which is one of the recurrent concerns of the residents (MoabitOnline [undated]).

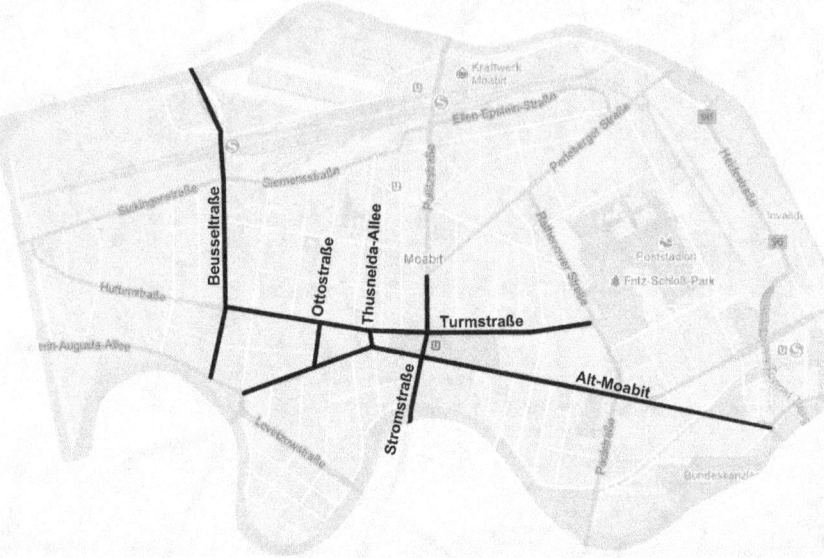

Figure 12: Streets map in the surroundings of *KTO*

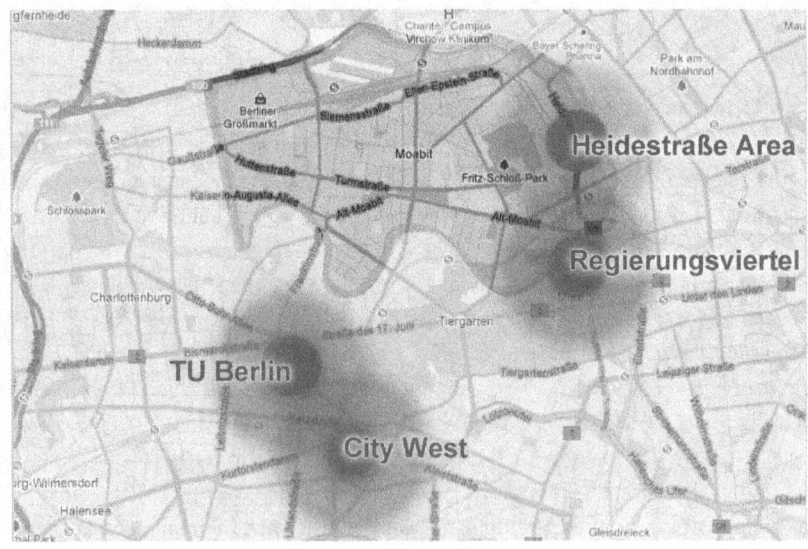

Figure 13: Urban poles of attraction in the surrounding of Moabit

A strong cultural and generational mix characterizes Moabit's population structure. Almost 45% of the 70,000 inhabitants of Moabit are citizens from diverse nationalities or with migration histories. That contributes to the diversity and richness of Moabit. The Development Index of Moabit fluctuates between low and medium (Amt für Statistik Berlin Brandenburg 2011, Bodenschatz et al. 2007, SenStadt 2009a). From the analysis of the Development Index Map of Berlin, the population living in the Northern part of Moabit is socially more disadvantaged (very low / low Development Index) than the population living in the Southern part (medium Development Index) (figure 14).

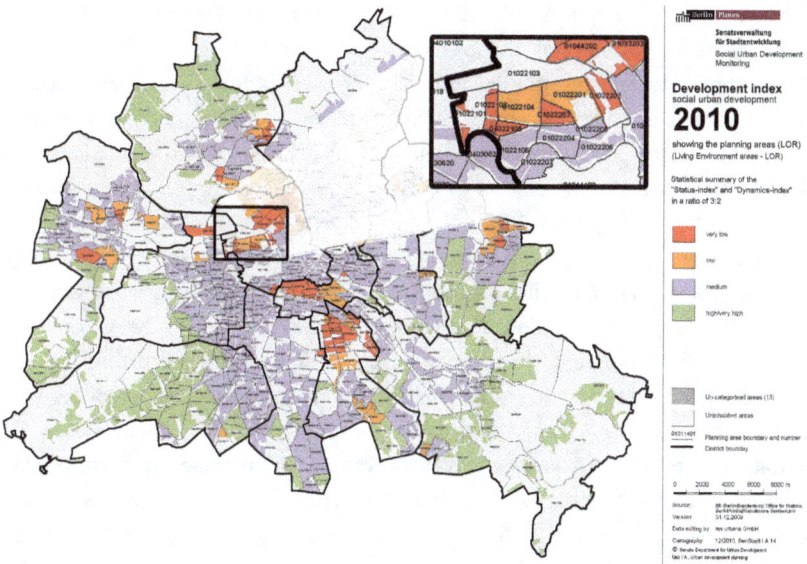

Figure 14: Development Index Berlin 2010

Moabit is one of the most socially disadvantaged neighborhoods of Berlin. Urban deficiencies are seen in Moabit, such as neglected public spaces and the low promotion of commercial activities, which are due to quasi non-existing investment in the urban development of the neighborhood over the last decade (Fenster 2001, SenStadt 2011a). The low investment in the renewal of urban infrastructure during the last decades led to the degradation and a loss of attractiveness of the public spaces in the areas around Turmstraße. The *KTO* green area has long been neglected. The high rate of individual motorized traffic along Turmstraße disturbs the neighborhood's atmosphere making it unpleasant for pedestrians and cyclers. While the heterogeneity and cultural diversity of the local businesses is identified as an opportunity for the local economy development, the lack of traders' network and the several vacant shops have affected the stability of the local economy on *Turmstraße*. The identification of these urban deficiencies and the low Development Index of Moabit led the Berlin administration to direct public efforts to enhance the infrastructures and services by implementing several urban renewal programs in the area. The concentration of public effort to revitalize disadvantaged neighborhoods in the city complies with the Leipzig Charter's overall goal to reduce social inequalities on the city level. Thus, Moabit benefits from European, federal and state programs, which aim to strengthen the economic development of the neighborhood, to enhance the living quality of the residents by renewing public infrastructure and balancing social inequalities. Some of these programs include *Stadtumbau West, Quartiermanagement Moabit West, Quartiersmanagement Moabit* Ost (figure 15). In addition to these programs, Turmstraße was selected as an area for the *AZ* Program in 2008 and as an urban renewal area (*Sanierungsgebiet*) in 2011. These two programs are complementary: *AZ* Program deals with the conceptual and financial issues of the focus area, while the urban renewal area defines the specific legal framework according to *BauGB* (Wilke Oct 2011). The main actions of the *AZ* Program are to improve public spaces, to re-structure the *KTO* green area, to re-design the traffic concept along Turmstraße, to strengthen the cultural and public services and to support development of the local economy. The overall goal of the *AZ* Program is to revitalize Turmstraße as an attractive commercial center for the neighborhood within ten years (Bezirksamt Mitte von Berlin et al. [undated], SenStadt 2011b). Since *AZ* Program supports the development of the Turmstraße area as a center of the Moabit neighborhood, the citizens benefiting from the outcomes of the program are not confined to the 14,000 residents living in the Program area (figure 16). To ensure integrated and coherent development of the neighborhood, a collaborative effort between several of the programs mentioned above is necessary. The coordinators of the urban development programs meet on a monthly basis for the so-called *AG Förderkulisse* to discuss the state of the diverse programs (Hurny Nov 2011).

Aktives Stadtzentrum Turmstraße Program

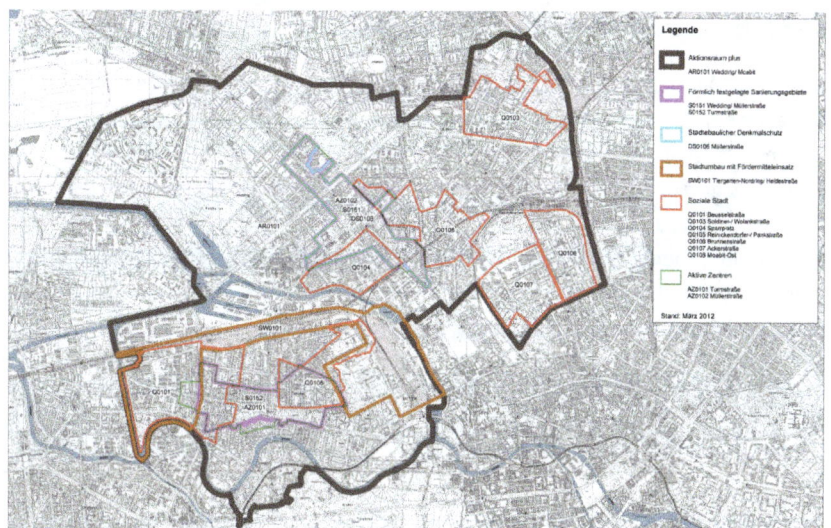

Figure 15: Urban renewal programs in Mitte

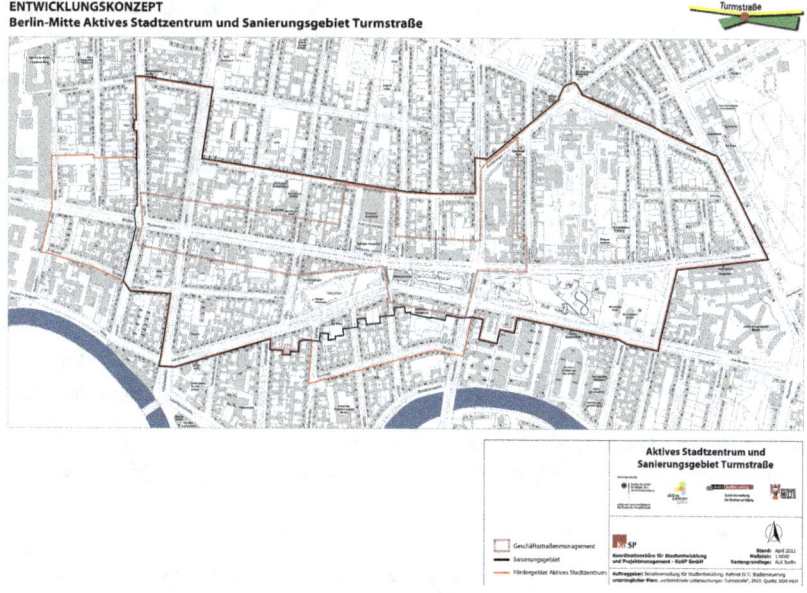

Figure 16: *Aktives Stadtzentrum* and Turmstraße 'urban renewal area'

5.3 Citizen participation in Moabit

Despite what Siebel (2010) claims regarding the low rate of citizen engagement in socially deprived neighborhoods (cf. chapter 4.2), the diverse actors shared similar statements expressing that citizens in Moabit are pro-active and have anchored their engagement for the neighborhood since the 1980s. Citizen participation in Moabit is rooted in the city-level rise of engagement in the 1980s and follows its own development, known as the 'Tiergarten citizen participation model', in the 1990s with the support of the political sector incarnated by Porath, former borough councilor for urban development in Tiergarten[7]. On the one hand, citizen participation was encouraged by financial and structural support from the Borough Administration Tiergarten. On the other, citizen entities had been politically independent to draft proposals, which were then discussed in assembly with politicians to define the actions and goals for the urban development of the neighborhood. Four citizen councils were elected in the late 1980s to represent the residents' interests in the areas that were potentially eligible for urban renewal programs. In the 1990s, the financial deficit of the state of Berlin caused a reduction in public expenditure and public support for citizen participation, which then had decreased. The administration reform of 2001, which redefined the borough's delimitation and set a new political direction, marked a turning point for citizen participation in Moabit. However, the citizen groups established during the 1980s and 1990s remain active in the area (Torka 2010).

SenStadt recognizes the city level success of the current neighborhood coordinators, such as the Neighborhood Management Program (*Quartiersmanagement*) and citizens' organizations, which promotes social dialogue and debate. They represent the so called "organizational motor" for the neighborhood network (SenStadt 2009, p. 24). The work the neighborhood coordinators do allows for the transfer of information and facilitates the link between the neighborhood actors and the Borough Administration. The several well-established citizens' organizations are recognized as crucial partners for the public administration of the borough of Mitte:

> "They collect the claim the right to discuss about urban restructuring processes. We find that wonderful and like to collaborate with these organizations" (SenStadt 2011a, p.44).

---

[7] Until 2001 Tiergarten was one of the 23 boroughs of Berlin. Moabit was one of the neighborhoods of Tiergarten borough. Since the administrative reform of 2001, the former boroughs of Tiergarten, Mitte and Wedding have been joined to the borough of Mitte.

Figure 17 summarizes the citizen entities that are recognized by the borough of Mitte as civil society partners. While an exhaustive list of the active citizen entities in Moabit is not the purpose of this chapter, some additional citizens' organizations and initiatives need to be included on this list to highlight the diversity and heterogeneity of citizens' initiatives, institutions and organizations in Moabit. These are: *Moabit ist Beste, Wem gehört Moabit, Zusammenschluss der Bürgerinnen und Bürger für einen respektvollen Umgang mit unseren Grünflächen, Silberahorn Initiative*.

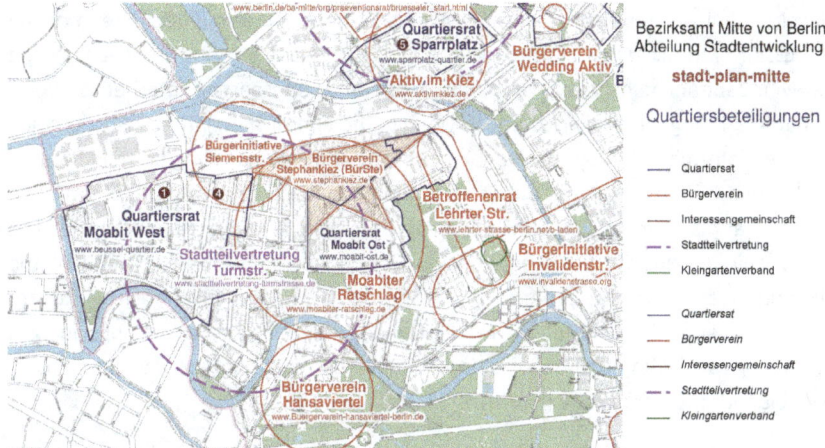

Figure 17: Neighborhood participation in Moabit

Due to their own specific concept, interest and organizational structure, citizen entities work with different forms of participation: information transfer, organization of protests and collaborative partnership, for example. Several ways of promoting transfer of knowledge and elaborating proposals to the public administration can be observed in Moabit. While the members of the *Lehrter Straße* are promoting a 'bottom-up' process by working independently of any institutional structure, other entities set their action on the development of social infrastructures by building cooperative partnership with the private sector, like *Bürgerverein Stefankiez (BürSte)* for instance. Yet, other citizen entities organize themselves to defend a specific interest in a determined time with a defined goal, such as *Siemensstraße Initiative,* which aims to defend the interests of residents against the design of the real estate development project taking place in their surroundings.

Another particularity of Moabit is the many forms of communication, which allows for a high level of information transfer and opinion sharing. Citizens of Moabit can get information through local newspapers: *Moabiter InselPost (Quartierszeitung Moabit West), LiesSte (BürSte), Ecke Turmstraße*[8] *(Aktives Stadtzentrum)*, etc. Additionally, a monthly forum takes place on the premises of the *Stadtschloss Moabit* Neighborhood Center. The meeting was originally initiated by Neighborhood Management West and Moabiter Ratschag (e.V.). *Stadtteilplenum* offers a space for discussion and debate between Moabit residents, merchants, public administrations, institutions and politicians on various topics related to the development of the Western part of Moabit. Citizens can also participate in online discussion forums. One of the most popular online platforms is MoabitOnline (www.moabitonline.de). It is a public, open and transparent Internet platform initiated and organized by citizens of Moabit. The aim of the platform is to provide updated information about the ongoing projects and actions taking place in Moabit, and to allow citizens to contribute to the debate in the online forum. MoabitOnline is a crucial platform of communication, which is open to every stakeholder and to every opinion, and it allows external actors to understand the evolution of the discourse regarding the projects and concerns that have taken place and are presently happening in Moabit. MoabitOnline is a useful database, providing a chronological documentation of citizens' concerns regarding the development of Moabit over the last decade (figure 18) (IRS 2011).

---

[8] *Ecke Turmstraße* is the newspaper of the *AZ* Program, which is published monthly since February 2011 and financed by the program.

Figure 18: MoabitOnline 'Space' for different communicative actions

5.4 Institutional Setting of Aktives Stadtzentrum Turmstraße Program

In this study, the notion of institutional setting within *AZ* Turmstraße Program is understood as the organization and interaction of the stakeholders involved in the planning and decision-making process of the program. During the fieldwork, the Borough Administration of Mitte, the Senate Administration of Berlin, the coordination office KoSP GmbH (KoSP, henceforth), and the members of the Stadtteilvertretung Turmstraße (*StV*) had been identified as stakeholders that constitute the institutional setting for the *AZ* Turmstraße Program. In the following chapter, the relevant planning and decision-making mechanisms in the framework of the *AZ* Program, and in Berlin's administration in general, are briefly outlined. Next, the stakeholder groups and their relevant functions are presented.

Administrative structure for AZ Program

Since *AZ* Program is a federally-based, a coordinating position, *Bundestransferstelle*, is responsible for carrying out and controlling the program on the federal level. Yearly, a workshop is organized to promote the practice exchange between cities and monitor the process for running the national program. At the Berlin state level, the collaboration between the boroughs and the Senate is based on close collaborative work between both administrations. *Landestransferstelle* assumes the role for coordinating and monitoring the administrative process of the program on the state level for all six *AZ* Programs in Berlin. A biannual meeting between the Senate and the involved boroughs is organized as a way to share experiences, discuss potential difficulties and monitor the program on the city level. As subordinates of the Senate, the boroughs involved have to provide financial and factual reports to the Senate to uphold the monitoring of the program implementation process concerning the completed and current projects. For future projects, the boroughs have to apply for financial funding from the Senate (complan Kommunalberatung 2011).

Coordinating Office of the AZ Turmstraße Program

To carry out and manage *AZ* Turmstraße Program and ensure the implementation of the vision defined by the Borough Administration in agreement with the Senate, the Borough Administration hires a coordinating office, which is responsible for managing the entire process of *AZ* Program and for representing the administration on site. Since January 2010, the coordination office for urban development and project management KoSP has been responsible for the coordination of the *AZ* Program. Besides several tasks that KoSP has to manage, it also acts as a coordinator for citizen participation. Although KoSP works under the authority of the Borough Administration, it plays the role of a so-called 'intermediate organization' within *AZ* Program, whereby its task is to link civil society with the public administration as a "bridge organization" (Bischoff et al 2005, p.195). Indeed, the public administration has to deal with the complexity of urban development: the interdisciplinary character of projects and the diversity of stakeholders involved in it. However, the current mistrust and misunderstanding between the public sector and civil society disturb the collaborative work. The goal of the 'intermediate organization' is therefore to bind "the different actors' spheres, the expert areas and the actions level (concept elaboration, project implementation) together" (Bischoff et al. 2005, p.196).

Citizen participation in AZ Program

Stadtteilvertretung (StV) – Neighborhood council

On the neighborhood level, *StV* is an elected group of citizen representatives. The organizational form of *StV* is based on the form of the residents' council founded in the 1980s. At that time, citizens became involved in the planning process of urban renewal programs and had been recognized as a residents' council (*Betroffenenvertretung*). The residents' council is legally anchored in *BauGB* Article 137 and ensures the rights of residents to a focused urban renewal area to be involved in the planning. The citizens decided to organize themselves under a citizens' council structure. Although *StV* does not hold direct legal power, the Borough Office of Mitte is committed to take into consideration the recommendations and positions of *StV*. To support the work of *StV*, the Borough Administration finances a venue where the representatives can meet and work, as well as an annual budget (3,000 Euros annually).

The current *StV* is composed of 27 members who were elected by citizens of Moabit in March 2011. There are two requirements to be eligible for membership: being older than 16 years of age and a resident of Moabit. The elections for *StV* occur every two years. The last election took place on the March 14, 2011 and was officially recognized by the Borough Office and the Borough Assembly of Mitte (Bezirksamt Mitte von Berlin 2011). The tasks and organization of *StV* are defined in the 'rules of procedure' (*Geschäftsordnung*) of *StV*, which is elaborated at the beginning of the mandate (cf. Appendix 2).

> "The elected *StV* for the *AZ* Program and renewal urban area *Turmstraße* participate in the planning and re-vitalization of the center of Moabit and ensures that the competences, the knowledge and the needs of the residents of Moabit are taken into account in the planning.
> The goal of the *StV* is to provide a relevant and innovative contribution for the enhancement of the attractiveness and residential quality.
> [...]
> The *StV* aims by its work to involve actively the citizens and to inform citizens about the ongoing projects and actions." (Stadtteilvertretung Turmstraße 2011, p.1)

Thematic workgroups (*Arbeitsgruppe (AG)*) are organized to treat specific issues such as green areas, named *AG Grün*, and a traffic concept for *Turmstraße*, named *AG Verkehr*. The aim of AGs is to expand citizen participation, since every citizen is encouraged to take part in the discussion and the elaboration of proposals, which are presented to the whole *StV* during the monthly public meetings that take place in Tiergarten City Hall in Moabit. These proposals are discussed between *StV* members and are eventually submitted to a vote. By subdividing the *StV's* process into workgroups, they enhance the democratic process of *StV* (Adner Nov 2011). Five members of *StV* – the so-called *StV* speakers (*StV Sprecher*) – are elected to represent *StV* and its positions in front of the administration during the monthly 'advisory council ', so-called *Beiratsrunde* (presented in the next sub-chapter) and report the results of the discussion to *StV* members (Stadtteilvertretung Turmstraße 2011).

Beiratsrunde (Advisory council)
Senate Administration, Borough Administration and *StV* speakers meet monthly in a closed meeting, moderated by KoSP. A journalist from the *AZ* Program newspaper *Ecke Turmstraße* is invited to join this meeting. The aim of the *Beiratsrunde* is to transfer information between the public sector and civil society: *StV* speakers report and explain the position of *StV* concerning the current projects, and the Borough Administration updates *StV* speakers about the progress and state of the projects as well as about the decision-making process. The *Beiratsrunde* is a space for common reflection and constructive collaboration towards consensus building. As KoSP mentioned during the meeting on November 8, 2011, the idea behind the meeting is to be open to changes (Beiratsrunde Nov 2011, Hurny Nov 2011). In 2010, the Borough Office of Mitte formally published the involvement of *StV* speakers in the *Beiratsrunde* and guaranteed a transparent transfer of information with *StV* during the planning and decision-making process for *AZ* Program (Bezirksamt Mitte von Berlin 2010).

Citizens' initiatives
Besides the established citizens' organizations, which aim to work on the development of Moabit in a long-term process, citizens' initiatives, or issue-based initiatives usually set to defend a specific issue, are key-actors in the development of the neighborhood. Two citizens' initiatives play a crucial role in the planning process of *KTO*: the *Silberahorn* initiative and the *Zusammenschluss der Bürgerinnen und Bürger für einen respektvollen Umgang mit unseren Grünflächen* initiative.
The *Silberahorn* initiative was founded in the summer of 2009 when a silver maple (*Silber-Ahorn*) in Moabit (on the corner of *Bochumerstraße* and *Dortmunderstraße*) was threatened by felling due to the construction of a new residential building. After this first action, the eight members of the initiative enlarged their action to protect

the green areas in Moabit. The initiative became strongly active in the planning process of *KTO* to protect healthy tree felling (Nake-Mann Dec 2011). The initiative *Zusammensschluss der Bürgerinnen und Bürger für einen respektvollen Umgang mit unseren Grünflächen (Respekt Gruppe*, henceforth*)* was founded in the summer of 2011 during the planning process of *KTO*. Before establishing the initiative, the future members had been involved in *AG Grün* of *StV*. During the working process, they were frustrated by the low influence of *AG Grün* in the planning process and decision-making. Since the work within *AG Grün* does not satisfy the position and interests of these citizens, they tried to act as individual citizens to defend their interests in front of the public administration. This was not efficient, which is why they finally decided to found an initiative that would be stronger and more readily heard by the public administration. The citizen initiative is composed of ten active members. The objective of the initiative is to reduce the amount of tree felling in the planning of *KTO* (Amannsberger Dec 2011).

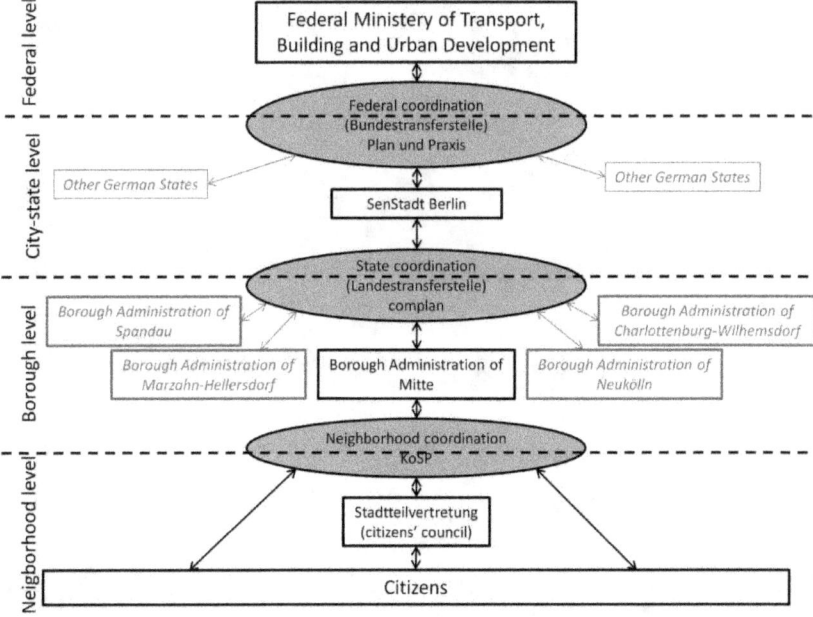

Figure 19: Structure of *AZ* Program from the federal to the neighborhood level

6 Planning process of Kleiner Tiergarten / Ottopark

6.1 Contextualization

One of the action areas of *AZ* Program is the restructuring of the *KTO* green area in the core of Moabit: *Kleiner Tiergarten / Ottopark* (*KTO*). The 6.2 hectares green area had been neglected during the past few decades and lost its attractiveness. The planning of *KTO* is subdivided in two planning sections: (1) *Ottopark* and western *Kleiner Tiergarten* and (2) eastern *Kleiner Tiergarten*. The implementation is subdivided into seven implementation sections (figures 20 and 21). The first two implementation sections have been under construction since October 2011. The five other sections are still in the planning process. The case study is focused on the planning process of the first planning section of *KTO*.

Figure 20: Overview map of the two *KTO* planning sections

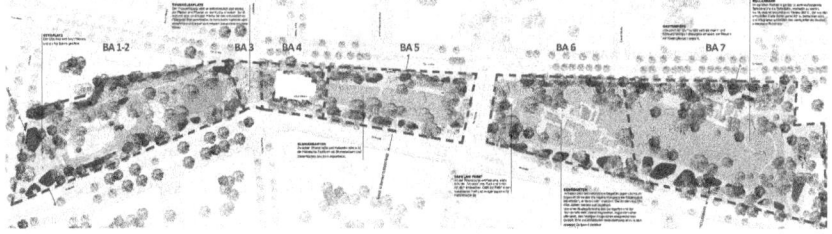

Figure 21: Overview map of the seven *KTO* implementation sections

Several weaknesses transformed the park into an unused and unconnected space. The park is missing amenities for different age groups; people with social integration problems (unemployed persons, homeless persons, and alcohol and drug addicts) occupy the park during the day and night, which discourages citizens and residents of Moabit from using the park. Nevertheless, the central location of the park in Moabit has the potential to strengthen communication and to provide a central meeting place, to encourage diverse social and cultural population groups to

exchange experiences and to encourage residents of Moabit to perceive the cultural diversity of their neighborhood as an advantage rather than as a weakness. The aim of this restructuring is to keep the green area attractive for the residents of Moabit and to enhance the image of the Turmstraße surroundings for neighborhood guests, as well as to strengthen the South-North connection within the neighborhood (Bezirksamt Mitte von Berlin et al 2010; KoSP 2010). The landscape concept was designed by Latz + Partner – a landscape architecture and urban planning company selected by competition (cf. chapter 6.3). The concept is based on three objectives:
- "Offers of diverse activities in the park for every user group
- Careful withdrawal of trees to regain the historic plan[9]
- Careful re-designing of the dense vegetation in an open and attractive additional usage area" (Bezirksamt Mitte von Berlin et al. 2010).

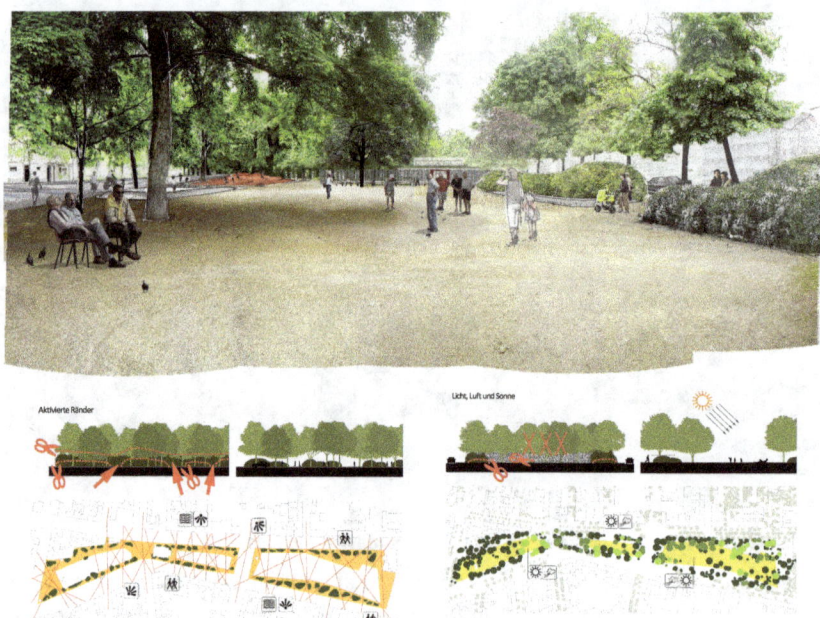

Figure 22: Latz+Partner Landscape Architecture Concept

---

9   Historic planning from Willy Alverdes in the 1950s.

6.2 Milestones of the planning

The project to re-arrange the *KTO* green area was proposed in the urban renewal concept for Turmstraße and presented to *SenStadt* for the selection of *AZ* areas in Berlin in 2008 as one of the action fields for the revitalization of the area (Bezirksamt Mitte von Berlin et al. [undated]). The planning process of *KTO* started in January 2010 with the publication of the competition requirements for landscape planning. The planning process is the subject of extensive citizen participation, which is carried out by the KoSP coordination office and is planned in close collaboration with *StV* Turmstraße.

Seven phases are identified in the entire planning process:

The first phase:	Elaboration of a landscape architecture concept for *KTO*
The second phase:	Collaborative work between *AG Grün* and the planners
The third phase:	Official participative events
The fourth phase:	A quest for a consensus on the tree felling issue
The fifth phase:	Citizen initiatives as leaders of the process
The sixth phase:	Political escalation
The seventh phase:	Political reversal

The following sections provide a chronological review of the planning process, phase by phase. Each phase is described with the intention of delivering a neutral statement of the situation. Then, interpretations for each phase allow for extracting relevant elements. The steps of the planning process and the relevant political and social events, which occurred during the process, are reported in the following table (figure 23).

	Events	Date
PHASE 1	Correspondence between AG Grün and the borough administration	16/12/2009
	Draft of tender documents for the landscape architecture competition	11/01/2010
	Suggestions from the Stadtteilvertretung for the tender documents drafting	15/01/2010
	Reward for theKTO landscape architecture concept	30/03/2010
	Public Open Air Event	19/06/2010
	Information Event to present the AG Grün	29/06/2010
	Public Information Meeting	05/07/2010
	Jury Session - Deliberation of the landscape architecture competition	06/07/2010
PHASE 2	Exhibition of the 16 landscape planning proposals	23/08/2010
	Cheklist for landscape planning	13/09/2010
	Presentation of the landscape concept to environment committee	14/09/2010
PHASE 3	Podium discussion	07/12/2010
	Childrens' Workshop	18/01/2011
	Citizens' Workshop	12/02/2011
	Presentation of revised plans	14/03/2011
	Stadtteilvertretung Election	14/03/2011
PHASE 4	1st public site tour	07/04/2011
	Report of Moabit citizens' opinion about the tree fellings in KTO	12/04/2011
	Appeal for a review of the landscape design regarding tree felling	23/04/2011
	Resolution of the StV to adopt the revised landscape architecture plans	02/05/2011
	Formal public planning procedure (*Planfeststellung*)	16/05/2011
	2d public site tour	17/05/2011
	Environment Committee Session	17/05/2011
	3d public site tour	23/05/2011
PHASE 5	New citizen initiative : Respekt Gruppe	01/07/2011
	Correspondence between citizen initiatives and BVV members	02/09/2011
	Request Drucksachen 2223/III BVV - Fraktion Bündnis 90/ Grüne	09/2011
	Resolution BVV Drucksachen 2223/III	16/09/2011
	Election of the House of Representative and Borough Assemblies in Berlin	18/09/2011
PHASE 6	Implementation start	26/09/2011
	Administration lawsuit (*Verwaltungsstreitsache*) - BUND	05/10/2011
	First tree fellings in Ottopark	06/10/2011
	Open letter from BUND and NABU	06/10/2011
	Citizens Demonstration	08/10/2011
	Rejection of the administration lawsuit - Verwaltungsgericht Berlin	11/10/2011
	Dissolution of AG Grün (StV)	24/10/2011
PHASE 7	BVV Session	27/10/2011
	Request Drucksache 2223/ III	04/11/2011
	Request Drucksache 0044/ IV	15/11/2011
	Request Drucksache 2223/ III	06/12/2011
	Request Drucksache 0070 / IV	06/12/2011
	BVV Session	15/12/2011
	Request Drucksache 0070 / IV	15/12/2011

Figure 23: Main events of the planning process

6.3 The first phase – Elaboration of a landscape architecture concept

Statement

The main objective of the first planning process – between October 2009 and July 2010 – was the selection of the landscape-planning concept in the framework of an architecture competition. The Senate commissioned the Borough Administration to oversee the competition process, which consisted of drafting specific requirements for the project, verification of the competitors' abilities to apply for the project, evaluation of the proposals and finally selection of the concept among the proposals.

From the early phase of the process, *AG Grün* of *StV* worked on the requirements that they wished the planners to address in the elaboration of the landscape concept. The public administration referred *AG Grün* to the external office, LA.BAR, which is responsible for the running of the competition process. The latter invited *AG Grün* to a constructive discussion about the possibilities for including *AG Grün*'s requirements in the competition documentation. The reviewed requirements of *AG Grün* were included in the annexes of the official competition documentation addressed to the planners on March 30, 2010 (AG Grün 2010, SenStadt 2010a).

In order to inform the citizens of the *KTO* project, *AG Grün* organized an informative open air event on June 19, 2010. The number of participants was estimated at around 50. Representatives of KoSP and of the public administration participated. On this day, some anonymous posters were hung in the park accusing *AG Grün* of *StV* of supporting a project in which tree felling would occur (MoabitOnline 2010). In reaction to this accusation, *StV* organized another public information event on June 29, 2010 to present the structure and the work of *StV* in the framework of *AZ* Program. A representative of *AG Grün* explained in the speech the role of *AG Grün* and encouraged the citizens to take part in the workgroup (*Arbeitsgruppe*) of *StV* (Nake-Mann 2010).

A few days later, on July 5, 2010, the 16 landscape planning proposals were presented to the public. This event was initiated by KoSP and took place one day before the jury meeting that decided the winner of the competition (Quartiersmanagement Moabit Ost 2010). The aim of this event was to collect the concerns of the citizens regarding the proposals of the competitors, which would be relevant for the selection of the winning concept by the jury the following day. The jury was composed of seven members: landscape planners, representatives of the Senate Administration and of the Borough Office of Mitte. Latz + Partner GbR – a

German landscape architecture office – won the competition and was selected for the elaboration of the planning for *KTO* (SenStadt 2010b). Among the several guests that witnessed the deliberation, *AG Grün* was represented.

Analysis – Interpretation

Since the first steps of a project are crucial for the entire process of the planning that follows, the analysis of the first phase is of special relevance, particularly for understanding of the interaction between the stakeholders involved. The main stakeholders in the decision-making for the selection of the landscape concept are *SenStadt* and the Borough Office and the Administration of Mitte (as decision-makers and veto-players), and *AG Grün* of *StV* and LA.BAR (as key stakeholders) (figure 24).

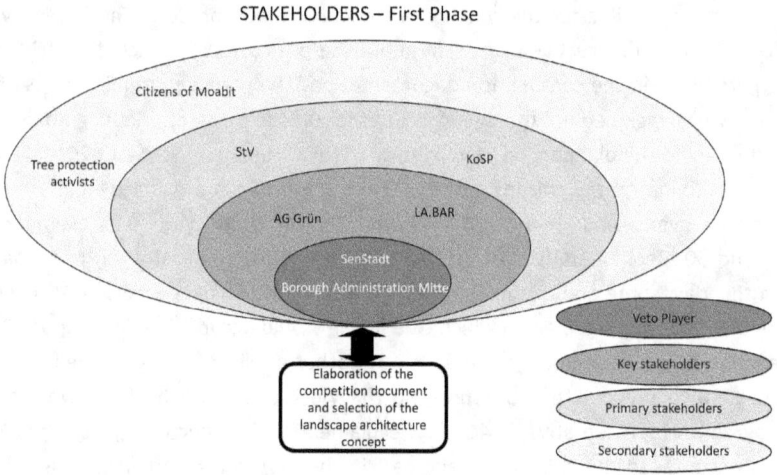

Figure 24: Categories of stakeholders involved in the first phase

From the analysis of the first phase – Elaboration of a landscape architecture concept – three relevant results can be extracted: (1) the lack of communication between the public administration and the citizens in the early phases leads to the citizens' frustration, (2) citizens show a high motivation to be involved in the planning process, and (3) the landscape architecture competition process does not allow for efficient citizen participation in the concept development.

(1) Lack of communication raises citizen frustration
During the first months after the election of *StV Turmstraße* (October 2009), the organization and interaction between the stakeholders of the institutional setting of *AZ* Program were not clearly defined. From the side of *AG Grün*, which were already operational to work on conceptual issues in the weeks following the *StV* election, several ambiguities needed to be clarified regarding the role and the degree of influence of *AG Grün* and the interaction with the other stakeholders involved in the planning of *KTO* (*AG Grün* 2009). At that point, the public administration did not clarify these specific issues and left the questions of *AG Grün* unanswered and referred them to LA.BAR (Nake-Mann Dec 2011a). This lack of communication in the early steps of the process led to a misunderstanding between *StV* and the Borough Administration, which fed frustration on the side of *StV* members regarding their role and influence in the institutional setting of *AZ* Program.

(2) Motivation and engagement of the citizens from StV
Since the election of the first *StV* in October 2009, the founded *AG Grün* has worked actively to fulfill its function as a 'field-expert' group in the institutional setting of *AZ* Program. In the early phase of the planning of *KTO*, *AG Grün* worked on the formulation of the citizens' requirements with the aim to include them in the editing of the competition documentation addressed to the planners in the framework of the landscape architecture competition. Although the communication between the Borough Administration and *AG Grün* had waned, *AG Grün* managed to address their expectations to the landscape planners through their constant perseverance and capacity to elaborate proposals and documentation. The collaborative interaction with LA.BAR contributed to the success of one of the first *AG Grün* interventions and allowed an exchange of information regarding the process of the competition. However, the organization of public events to inform citizens about the institutional setting of *AZ* Program, and especially the planned concept of the *KTO* restructuring project, demonstrated the seriousness and motivation of the elected members of *StV* to encourage the residents of Moabit to engage in the development of their neighborhood.

(3) Low degree of participation in the competition
In a formal architecture competition process, the space allocated for citizen participation is relatively small. The anonymous process of the applications prevents

a direct interaction between planners and citizens for the elaboration of the concept (Gruber and Stegmeier Dec 2011). Nevertheless, *AG Grün* requirements were included in the annexes of the competition documentation and informative events were organized. Despite the fact that members of *AG Grün* were invited as guests in the deliberative jury meeting, they did not take part in the deliberative decision-making.

6.4 The second phase - Communication between AG Grün and the planners

Statement

Between July and December 2010, several informative events and meetings took place in Moabit addressing the citizens; at the Borough Assembly, discussions took place among politicians. On August 23, 2010, an exhibition of the 16 landscape planning proposals which had competed for the planning of *KTO* was opened for two weeks. This exhibition was an informative event, since the winner of the competition had already been selected.

On October 14, 2010, the planners presented their concept to the Environment Committee of the Borough Assembly of Mitte during the monthly public meeting. This presentation, initiated by KoSP, fostered a discussion between politicians, citizens and planners. At the same time, *AG Grün* continued to work on proposals for the planning and established contact with the landscape planners. A site tour in *KTO* initiated by *AG Grün* on October 26, 2010 indicates that there was a willingness on the part of the planners to collaborate with *AG Grün*. The latter wrote two reports to define criteria and to establish their positions and transmitted the reports to the planners.

Analysis – Interpretation

Between July and December 2010, the interaction between the actors stayed on an informative level. Nonetheless, *AG Grün* worked actively in collaboration with the planners. The planners showed an open stance and demonstrated a willingness to include citizens' opinions and requirements in the planning as far as the technical and conceptual framework would allow. This collaboration was constructive for both sides: the planners were informed of specific issues by the citizens and *AG Grün* was informed of the technical and planning process challenges from the point of view of the planners. Apart from information transfer, the collaborative work between the planners and the members of *AG Grün* contributed to building a trusting relationship between the actors (Adner Nov 2011). This statement highlights the established partnership between *AG Grün* and the planners on the local level and their autonomy from the public administration.

6.5 The third phase – Official participative events

Statement

During the third phase of the planning, a participative process geared for the citizens of Moabit was initiated by KoSP. Four main participative events occurred between December 2010 and March 2011. To encourage citizens to participate, KoSP spread flyers and posters in Moabit to inform them about the planning of the green area and to invite citizens to join the participatory workshops (Bezirksamt Mitte von Berlin et al. 2010).

First participatory event – Podium discussion
The first event took place on December 7, 2010 in the form of a podium discussion moderated by KoSP. The podium had been composed of representatives of *SenStadt*, the Borough Office, the Borough Administration and the landscape planners. Around 60 participants came to the two-hour long meeting, which took place at a venue on Ottostraße. The aims of this meeting were to present the current landscape concept, and to open the discussion to collect remarks and recommendations for the elaboration of the detailed planning. According to the meeting report, the participants interacted actively in the discussion and addressed conceptual proposals regarding the motorized traffic around the park and extremely detailed technical and architectural proposals. Topics such as the closing of *Thusnelda-Allee*[10] and the tree felling were discussed in an emotionally charged atmosphere as the report suggests:

---

[10] The original idea in the development concept of *AZ Turmstraße* Program suggested converting Thusnelda-Allee to a public place free of motorized vehicles (Bezirksamt Mitte von Berlin et al. [undated]). In the 'traffic urban development plan' (*Stadtentwicklungsplan Verkehr*), the expansion of the tramway from Nordbahnhof to Turmstraße is foreseen for the coming years (SenStadt 2011c). One of the third options for the tramway is crossing Thusnelda-Allee which compromises the closure of Thusnelda-Allee (SenStadt 2011a).

"A large number of participants took vehemently position for the closing of the *Thusnelda-Allee* [...] *The intervention on vegetation is* perceived *essentially very negatively."* (KoSP 2010, p.6)

From the podium's side, Gothe – the Borough Councilor for Urban Development at this time – presented the information that the number of trees that would be felled had been one of the criteria in the evaluation of the landscape competition. The participants asked to have participation and information early on about the tree felling. KoSP announced a future public meeting with an expert on trees, which would be organized in March 2011 (KoSP 2010).

Figure 25: Podium discussion on December 7, 2010

Second participatory event – Workshop with young people
The second step of the participative process was a workshop for children and young people between the ages of 12 and 20 to develop ideas for the design of the playground in the west side of the park. Moabiter Ratschlag e.V. was commissioned by the Borough Administration Mitte to organize and moderate the workshop.

Moabiter Ratschlag e.V. is a well-established citizens' institution in Moabit. Longtime experience with young citizen participation allows Moabiter Ratschlag e.V. to reach the target groups for the workshop and work in collaboration with schools and associations for children and young people. To inform and encourage children and young people to take part in the workshop, 300 invitation flyers were distributed (figure 26). Sixty children took part in the workshop. The participants were representative of the population structure in the area – 50% of the children had a migration history and came from socially disadvantaged families. After developing their ideas for the playground area in groups, all the participants met to present their results to other groups and to the planners. The results of the workshop have been summarized by Moabiter Ratschlag e.V (Moabiter Ratschlag e. V. 2011, Homann Nov 2011).

Figure 26: Moabiter Ratschlag e.V. Flyer

Third participatory event – Citizens' workshop
The third step of the participative process consisted of a workshop with citizens of Moabit. The aims of the seven-hour workshop, conducted on February 12, were to present the current state of the first planning section, *Ottopark* and western *Kleiner Tiergarten*, to collect requirements and ideas from citizens as well as to lead a discussion between citizens and planners. Informed about the workshop by the distribution of flyers, 60 participants took part in the workshop moderated by KoSP. From the experts' side, Latz + Partner, the landscape planners, presented the

planning for *KTO*; a tree expert presented the results of its study from October 2010. The Borough Office had been represented by Gothe and representatives of the Borough Administration took part in the workshop as well. The results of the discussion focused on the vegetation concept and the desired amenities. This direct interaction between citizens and planners allowed for the clarification of controversial questions and the explanation of technical constraints, which had limited the inclusion of some citizens' requirements in the concept. The workshop led to an identification of the challenges and problems from the point of view of the citizens. The major challenging topics that came up during the workshop were the functional transformation of *Thusnelda-Allee* and the tree felling. The results of the workshop are summarized in the report of KoSP (KoSP 2011).

Fourth participatory event – the feedback from the workshops
The last step of the participatory planning was the presentation of the revised planning based on the results of the workshops. The presentation occurred three weeks after the workshop, on March 14, and was limited to an informative presentation without the possibility for modifications or re-adjustments (KoSP 2011, Adner Nov 2011, and Hurny Nov 2011). On May 2, 2011, *StV* publicly took an official position in favor of the reviewed planning of Latz + Partner:

> "The *StV* Turmstraße welcomes and supports the current planning of the landscape architecture office Latz + Partner" (Stadtteilvertretung Turmstraße 2011a).

Analysis – Interpretation

The most relevant adaptations of the concept and of the detailed plans corresponding to citizens' needs and expectations occurred during the third phase of the planning. The participative events had been organized by KoSP and addressed the citizens of Moabit. The key stakeholders in the development of the planning are the citizens as field experts and the planners as technical experts. The Senate and the Borough Administration remain veto-players (figure 27).

Planning process of Kleiner Tiergarten / Ottopark

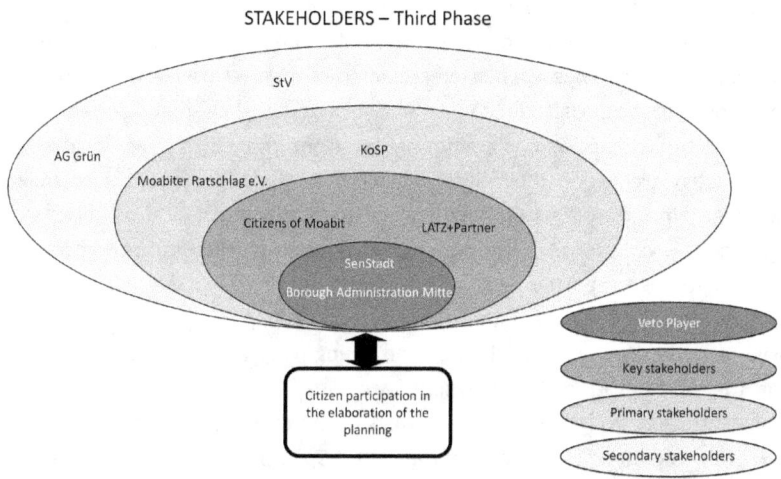

Figure 27: Categories of stakeholders involved in the third phase

The analysis of the participative events allows for detecting areas for improvement: (1) in the communication strategy to encourage citizens to participate, and (2) in the organization of the participative events.

(1) Communication strategy to provide an incentive for citizen participation
A communication strategy to encourage citizens to participate that the coordination office KoSP had relied on employed diverse means of communication: flyers, posters, internet platforms, etc. The average participation rate was 60 participants in the several events and is considered highly disappointing for a project which concerns the whole neighborhood of Moabit (with around 70,000 inhabitants). Although the members of *AG Grün* and *StV* participated in the workshop as citizens and not as members of the institutional setting of *AZ* Program, their role in the preparation of the events appears to be crucial. As defined in the 'rules of procedure' of *StV*, one of the functions of *StV* members is to involve the citizens actively and to inform them about ongoing projects and activities. In these terms, *AG Grün* members could contribute to the communication strategy design in a closer collaboration with KoSP and play a role of 'disseminators' to encourage citizens to participate in the events.

(2) Organization of the participative events
From the evaluation of the diverse stakeholders interviewed during the fieldwork, the workshops have been perceived as constructive: the citizens could express their concerns and proposals directly to the planners, while the planners had the possibility to collect valuable information from the citizens as 'field–experts'. Constructive discussion took place in which the participants had a possibility to exchange different points of view, and to learn about technical or administrative constraints encountered in the planning. Two relevant critiques of the participative events had been reported by the interviewed stakeholders. The first one concerns the inappropriate date for the workshop for young people and children. The planning workshop with the children and young people had also been constructive and the moderators of the workshop, Moabiter Ratschlag e.V., took part in the following events to represent the interests of the target group. Moabiter Ratschlag e.V. evaluated the entire process of the workshop as positive. Still, January is not the most appropriate month to conduct a workshop on landscape planning with children and young people due to the cold weather and early darkness, which limit the efficiency of the work site (Homann Nov 2011). The second critical point concerns the lack of possibilities for the citizens to enhance the planning review after the workshop. The interviewed stakeholders agreed that the feedback from the workshop had been limited to the presentation of the revised planning by the planners without the possibility for citizens to interact (Adner Nov 2011, Hurny Nov 2011, and Bezirksamt Mitte von Berlin 2011a).

Figure 28: Citizens' Workshop on February 12, 2011

6.6 The fourth phase – A quest for a consensus on the tree felling issue

Statement

Since the beginning of the planning, the tree felling has been the most controversial issue. According to Latz + Partner's planning of the first to the fifth implementation sections – from Ottostraße to Stromstraße – around 100 of the approximately 400 existing trees are to be felled.

During the podium discussion in December, KoSP announced that a public site tour will be expected with a tree expert to discuss the vegetation concept. The tour took place on April 7, 2011. According to the testimony of participants, environmental activists from other boroughs of Berlin attended the tour and disturbed the discussion. The results of the tour did not correspond to the expectations of the citizens (Adner Nov 2011, Nake-Mann Dec 2011).

On April 12, members of the *Silberahorn* initiative published a report summarizing the opinions of Moabit citizens regarding the tree felling and reproached the public administration for not getting information about the tree felling to residents (Firouzi et al 2011). In addition to this report, on April 23, the *Silberahorn* initiative appealed to the politicians, including the Senator for Urban Development, Mayor of the Borough Mitte, Councilor for Urban Development Mitte and fractions of the Borough Assembly Mitte. In the appeal, the initiative pleaded for the conservation of the 'healthy' trees, proposed alternatives and invited the politicians for an additional site tour in order to understand the concern of the initiative before the Environment Committee meeting scheduled on May 17, 2011. In the conclusion of the appeal, the initiative warned politicians about potential social conflicts if the current planning was not reconsidered:

> "Please, give additional time to the planners and decision-makers for reflection and organize this reflection in another form to avoid that the re-arrangement of the *Kleiner Tiergarten* lead to a social confrontation." (Silberahorn et al. 2011, p.3)

This second site tour took place on the May 17, one hour before the session (Nake-Mann Dec 2011). During the discussion process between planners, citizens and politicians, 11 trees, which should originally have been felled, are conserved. On the 23rd of May, a site tour with *AG Grün* and the planners, as well as representatives of the public administration, took place in order to discuss the tree issue specifically. The result of the two site tours (on May 17 and 23) was the conservation of 16 trees. However, some members of *AG Grün* were unsatisfied with the result and the process of negotiation. Internal discordances among active members were starting to be felt in *AG Grün* (Amannsberger Dec 2011).

Analysis – Interpretation

In April and May 2011, the topic of tree felling became a highly controversial issue in the *KTO* restructuring plan, which is not unusual in the restructuring of green areas in German dense urban areas. Several stakeholders aimed to be active to overcome the conflict: politicians, KoSP, planners, tree experts, *AG Grün* and citizens' initiatives. The interaction between the stakeholders appears to occur in a spontaneous and unstructured process without common agreement between the stakeholders on the form of communication which would be used to achieve the aims. Several site tours were organized: one by the coordination office, one by the *Silberahorn* initiative and one by *AG Grün*. *AG Grün* and the *Silberahorn* initiative, who shared the concern for reducing the felling of healthy tree applied different strategies to achieve their goal: while *AG Grün* worked directly with the planners and stayed within the institutional setting of *AZ Program*, the *Silberahorn* initiative turned to the Environment Committee of the *BVV* and raised the debate to the political level.

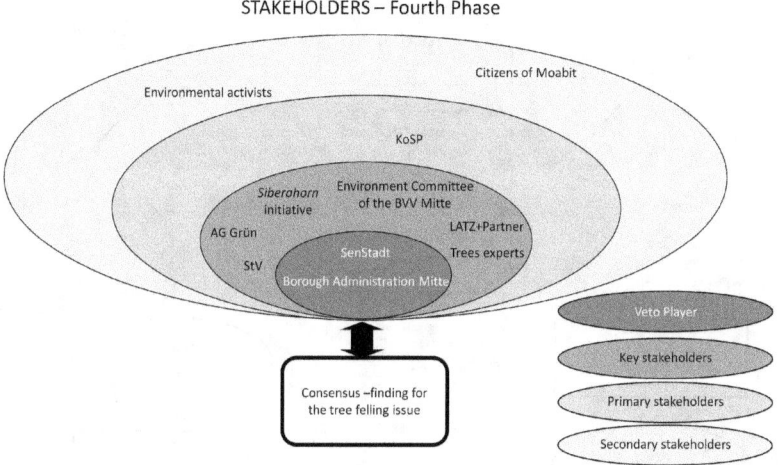

Figure 29: Categories of stakeholders involved in the fourth phase

The results of the site tour on May 23, 2011 were considered as consensus by the Borough Administration, by the Borough Office and by the *StV*. Nevertheless, members of *AG Grün* did not accept these results as consensus. Figure 30 summarizes the two interpretations of the process: (i) rise of frustration from the citizens' initiatives side, and (ii) assessment for achieving consensus on part of the public administration.

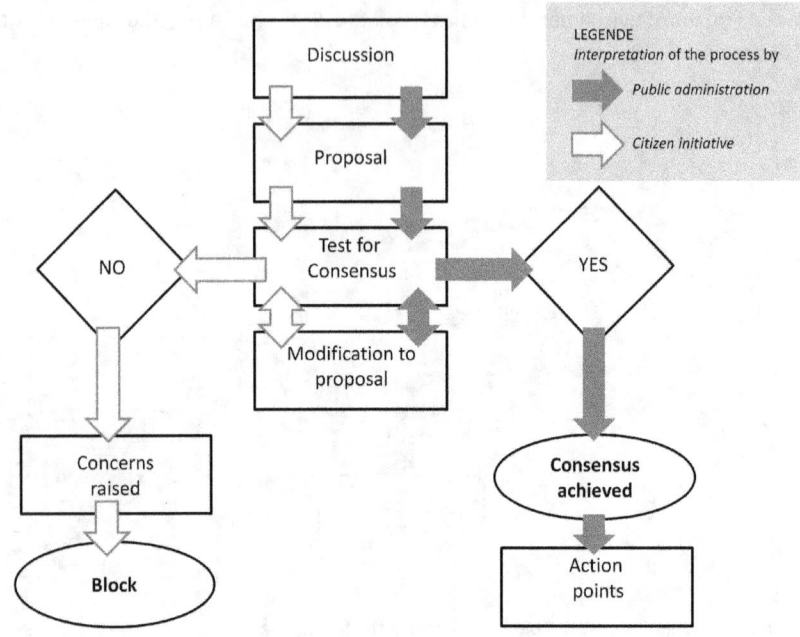

Figure 30: Interpretation of the consensus building process by the stakeholders

This phase of the planning strongly affects the structure of *StV*. The rise of discordance within *AG Grün* discredited its function as a 'specialist advisers' group for *StV* decision-making. Despite the intern conflicting situation, the *StV* voted the resolution to support the elaborated plans for *KTO*. This action impacted the legitimacy of *StV* negatively.

The form of communication applied to resolve the conflict situation does not appear appropriate at this stage of the process. The conflict about the tree issue had been perceptible since the first phase of the concept's formation. The rise of protests in this phase of the planning could have been solved through the organization of an appropriate communication form. At this time of the planning, the different stakeholders were open to a consensus finding process. One of the appropriate communication tools for consensus finding is the organization of a round table with the aim of presenting proposals to the decision-makers (cf. chapter 4.3 and chapter 7.3).

6.7 The fifth phase – Citizens' initiatives as leaders of the process

Statement

During the process of consensus finding for the tree felling issue, members of *AG Grün* were disappointed by the strategy applied by the coordinator of *AG*. The work of *AG Grün* suffered from this internal discordance of opinions. Engaged citizens in *AG Grün* had not recognized *StV* as a representative of their opinions. In July 2011, members of *AG Grün* decided to form the *Respekt Gruppe* initiative. Since the two active initiatives had not been heard either by *StV* or by the Borough Administration, *Respekt Gruppe* and the *Silberahorn* initiatives had voiced their concerns to the political fractions of *BVV* and elevated the debate to the borough level. On September 2nd, in an open letter to the *BVV* fractions, the *Silberahorn* initiative pleaded for a more expensive process with more advanced participation for the planning of the western *Kleiner Tiergarten* (Silberahorn 2011). The *Respekt Gruppe* initiative organized a petition against the tree felling in *Ottopark* in order to demonstrate to the politicians that "they are the majority" (Amannsberger Dec 2011). They collected 2800 signatures in four weeks and presented their results to the politicians. On September 16, 2011, two days before the election of the House of Representatives and the Borough Assemblies of Berlin, the Borough Assembly unanimously set a requirement for a mediation process to solve the tree felling conflict between politicians, planners, administrations and citizens' initiatives. It also agreed on a moratorium of the tree felling until consensus is reached (BVV Mitte 2011).

Analysis – Interpretation

A few days before the election of the Berlin parliament, the *Respekt Gruppe* initiative provided the 2800 signatures of residents opposed to the tree felling to the fractions of *BVV* and called for a moratorium on the tree felling and a mediation process to solve the conflict. The pressure of losing voters' support influenced the political fractions of *BVV* in their decision to support the citizen initiatives. On September 16, all the political fractions of the Borough Assembly voted for a moratorium on the tree felling, which meant postponing the start date for implementation, which was expected to begin two weeks later, to an undetermined date. Premeditated or not, the organization of the petition during the election campaign was a successful strategy for the citizen initiatives to convince politicians to support their actions. If the actions of the citizens' initiatives have been interpreted as excessive by some stakeholders, the enthusiasm in the planning process of *KTO* that they generated in the civil society and on the political level is remarkable and shows their ability to make use of the resources available to them for their cause.

6.8 The sixth phase – Political escalation

Statement

Despite BVV's commitment to a moratorium on tree felling, the commencement of tree felling and restructuring of *KTO* – from *Ottostraße* to *Thusnelda-Allee* – started on October 6, 2011. The Borough Office legitimated its position based on May 23, 2011 *StV* agreement regarding the amount of trees which could be felled. The citizens' initiatives reacted to this action with the support of environmental associations – *Bund für Umwelt und Naturschutz Deutschland* (BUND) and *Naturschutzbund Landesverband Berlin* (NABU) – and appealed to the Administrative Court to establish jurisdiction. On October 5, they filed at the Administrative Court of Berlin

> "To forbid with immediate effect the felling work in *Ottopark* until the mediation for conservation of the trees is summoned and a result is committed." (Verwaltungsgericht Berlin 2011, p.4)

Furthermore, the environmental association BUND and NABU addressed an open letter to *Die Linke* party of *BVV* Mitte to denounce the contradictory attitude of the Borough Office regarding the Borough Assembly's decision concerning the tree felling moratorium:

> "Now the trust in the Borough Office and its responsibility in the long-term has been shaken [...] It is not understandable to us how a democratic legitimate assembly through its own executive institution – here the Borough Office – can be nullified [...] For the future, the two nature and environmental associations require an early and practice-oriented planning and involvement of all actors. Moreover, moratorium and resolutions have to be credible; they should not be a pure appeasement nor bring wrong expectations"(BUND and NABU 2011, pp.1-2).

On October 8, 2011, the Administrative Court rejected the demand (Verwaltungsgericht Berlin 2011). Protests were organized to stop the tree felling; the police had to intervene. A demonstration was initiated on October 10 at the city hall of Tiergarten, in front of *Ottopark*. Newspapers reported the debate on the borough and city level (Berliner Zeitung 2011, Jacobs and Heine 2011, Fiedler 2011).

Environmental citizen organizations took part in the debate in an online forum (Landwehrkanal-blog 2011, NABU 2011). On the MoabitOnline platform, citizens participated actively in the debate (MoabitOnline 2011). During the process, the cohesion and integrity of *AG Grün* was strongly challenged. Members of the citizen initiatives used *AG Grün* as a way to channel their own interests. By refuting publicly *StV*'s decision under the name of *AG Grün*, the members of *AG Grün* broke the rules established in the 'rules of procedure' of *StV*, which stated that *AGs* are submitted to the decision of *StV*:

> "The *AGs* are bound to the resolution of the *StV*. They are not autonomous.
> The position of the AGs can exclusively be made public by the speakers of the *StV*, by the AG Publication or by the coordinators of the AGs.
> Any position, which contradicts the resolution of the *StV* in word or in sense, can be communicated externally on behalf of an AG."[11] (Stadtteilvertretung Turmstraße 2011)

During the *StV* session on October 24, 2011, the members of *StV* decided to dissolve the *Grün* (Stadtteilvertretung Turmstraße 2011b).

Interpretation - Analysis

Although the politicians had reported the concerns of the citizens in front of *BVV*, and voted unanimously on a resolution to call for an additional participative round to solve the conflicting situation, the results of their effort were inefficient and less consequential than the field-work of the initiatives and of *StV* that was observed during the fourth phase of planning. However, the decision of the Borough Office to begin implement despite the decision of the Borough Assembly, and despite the strong divergence of opinions within civil society, strengthened the frustration of citizens and increased the gap between citizens and decision-makers. This situation highlights the limitation of the representative democracy on the Borough level, which is controlled by political powers at the expense of the citizens of Moabit (who could have been represented by *StV*). Even so, the necessity to dissolve *AG Grün* points to the vulnerability of *StV* to powerful activists. In this context, *StV* failed in its charge as a representative for the community.

---

[11] See Appendix 3.

Figure 31: Information board for the *KTO* restructuring tagged by tree protecting activists

6.9 The seventh phase – Political reversal

Statement

On November 4, 2011, Gothe formalized the Borough Office's position regarding the moratorium on tree felling and the following planning process of *KTO* by an official response (*Drucksache*) addressed to the party Bündnis 90/Die Grünen of BVV Mitte. The argumentation had been based on a report issued to the Department of Transport and Green Area of the Borough Office, which provided a list of issues again advocating for a moratorium on the tree felling and a mediation process for the planning of *Ottopark* (Bezirksamt Mitte von Berlin 2011b). In the argumentation list the two following points are mentioned:

> "A construction contract is already concluded. The contract is in place after half a year of planning and intensive citizen participation process (supported by the *StV* as elected assembly of representative of Moabit citizens) and after a tender public procedure [...]

The financial damages without revised planning would be around 170.000 to 200.000 Euros until December. The financial damages with revised planning are difficult to estimate, they would be at least around 250.000 Euros. The Berlin Senate is opposed to allocating a public fund to the AZ Program. No funds are available for this process." (Bezirksamt Mitte von Berlin 2011c, pp.1-2)

Regarding the tree felling issue of the western *Kleiner Tiergarten*, a round table was expected with the aim to discuss the planning and tree felling concept in a decision-making process, which consists of several steps (Bezirksamt Mitte von Berlin 2011b). On December 6, 2011, Carsten Spallek – successor of Ephraim Gothe as the head of the Borough Council for Urban Development after the September elections – responded to the request for a mediation process for the restructuring of *KTO* by print:

"The Borough Office considers that a mediation process [...] and a round table are not necessary. On the contrary, the Borough Office is concerned about the negative consequences that a focus on the issue of tree felling could have on the motivation of the citizens to participate in the urban renewal program '*Aktives Zentrum und Sanierungsgebiet Turmstraße*'. The Borough Office is focused on continuing the ongoing planning and a participative process in an intensive form and to ensure a transparency in public work and a democratic citizen participation in the planning of *KTO*." (Bezirksamt Mitte von Berlin 2011d, p. 3)

The reversal of position led to a debate regarding the political willingness for citizen participation on the borough level (SPD Alt Moabit 2011). Despite the political debate and citizens' protests, KoSP further organized three meetings on site to inform citizens on the progress of the construction between November and December 2011.

Analysis – Interpretation

By rejecting the decision of the former Urban Development Department to organize a round table to solve the conflict regarding the tree felling issue in the western *Kleiner Tiergarten*, Spallek expressed a new approach regarding citizen participation. This political change led to a turn in the orientation of the Borough Office regarding participation and led to a conflicting political debate on the borough level (SPD Alt Moabit 2011). This situation confirms that participative practices strongly depend on political willingness. Political changes appear to be a threat for sustainable neighborhood governance. This can also be interpreted as a sign of crisis for representative democracy on the borough level; it speaks in favor of more autonomous and legally defined participative local governance.

6.10 Stakeholders and their interactions

Figure 32 summarizes the interaction between the stakeholders during the planning process of the first section of *KTO*. This chart highlights the channels that the citizens used in order to reach the decision-makers' sphere, and by this to influence the decision-making process.

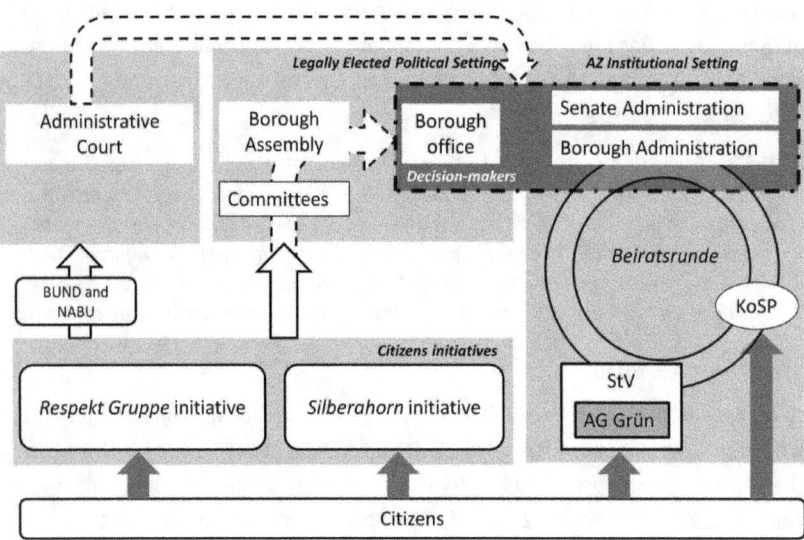

Figure 32: Citizens channels to reach the decision-making sphere in *KTO* restructuring planning

7 Citizen participation as local experts

The previous chronologically presented critical review of the planning process allows for extracting the elements which will support the argument of this study. Based on these observations and corresponding interpretations, areas for improvement are identified and submitted for proper study with the aim of answering the question: *'How do communication tools enable efficient citizen participation?'*

From the analysis of the seven phases, four weaknesses of the planning process have been identified:
- The low level of citizen participation in the development of the landscape concept
- The inappropriate time schedule for the workshop with children and young people
- The lack of a 'feed-back' workshop to improve the reviewed plan
- The inappropriate form of conflict solving strategies regarding the tree felling issue

The following chapter will present a critical review of the participatory process of the planning and propose alternative communication forms, which are assumed to be more appropriate in the case of the *KTO* restructuring.

According to the analysis of the available documentation and reports of the participative planning, as well as of the testimony of the key-stakeholders, the level of citizens' involvement during the planning process is evaluated. Based on the ranking of the level of citizens' involvement referred in the *Handbuch Partizipation* (cf. chapter 4.2) the citizens' involvement in the key steps of the planning process is assessed in six different categories: no involvement, information, participation, involvement in decision-making, decision-making, self-governance. Figure 33 presents the level of citizens' involvement and illustrates the potential space for improvement (arrows). These interpretations are derived from the results of the analysis of the seven phases.

Key-steps of the participative process	Target groups	Level of involvement				
		Information	Participation	Participation in decision-making	Decision-Making	Self-governance
Elaboration of the landscape architecture concept	Citizens	●┈┈⇢				
Elaboration of the landscape architecture concept	AG Grün		●			
Podium Discussion	Citizens	●				
Workshop with children and young people	Children and young people		●			
Workshop with citizens	Citizens		●			
Presentation of the revised planning	Citizens	●┈┈┈⇢				
Solving the conflicting issue of tree felling	AG Grün Citizens' iniatives		●┈┈┈⇢			

Figure 33: Citizens' involvement in key steps of the planning process and areas for improvement

7.1 Citizen participation in the concept elaboration

In terms of the way in which the concept of the restructuring of the green area had been developed, the choice of a landscape architecture competition is questionable. Since citizen participation is a crucial aspect in the management process of *AZ Program*, a communicative form of concept building, which would allow for greater citizen participation, is more appropriate. This issue has been mentioned by key stakeholders during the interviews. Members of the former *AG Grün* questioned the process of the concept's formation in the early phase (Nake-Mann Dec 2011). Retrospectively, the representative of the Borough Administration considered that an improvement in the planning process could have been to involve citizens in the concept's elaboration before the design of the preliminary plan by the landscape architecture office (Hurny Nov 2011). The participation of citizens in the development of the concept ensures several advantages, which contribute to the enhancement of the entire process:

- By involving citizens in the early phase, the rate of participation in the consecutive planning stage rises and helps to identify conflicting issues at the beginning of the process
- A collaborative work in the early phase contributes to the establishment of trusting relationships between the public administration and citizens, and enhances the acceptance of the project
- By integrating the citizens' needs and expectations in the development of the design, the quality of the planning improves and the planners save time in future planning steps by avoiding having to make fundamental changes, which can be necessary in the later phases.

The communication form *Planning for Real* seems to be an appropriate tool in this case. *Planning for Real* is designed to reach a large, diverse part of the population and it aims to produce documentation, which provides the necessary information for planners to elaborate the concept and plans. *Planning for Real*'s specialty is for reaching citizens in public spaces and elaborating a model by appealing to citizens' creativity, while at the same time collecting realistic proposals. *Planning for Real* is based on a direct interaction between citizen leaders who organize the process, and field-expert citizens who live in the area. *Local Ideas Action* and *Action Planning* are two other suitable alternative communication tools which could be also applied in this context (cf. chapter 4.3).

7.2 Enhancement of the official participative events

A preliminary understanding of the constraints that interfere with the arrangement of the time table for participatory planning is necessary for a critical review of the participatory process. The empirically-driven theory shows the importance of scheduling citizen participation and the implementation of the project as close as possible (cf. Chapter 4.4). The legal framework of planning itself, as well as the formal tender procedure, need to be taken into account for appropriate time management while developing the participation process. Contract conditions also play a crucial role in time management, as well as the availability of financial resources since a limited budget is allocated yearly for *AZ Turmstraße* Program. The official closure of the participatory planning is determined based on the date implementation begins (figure 34).

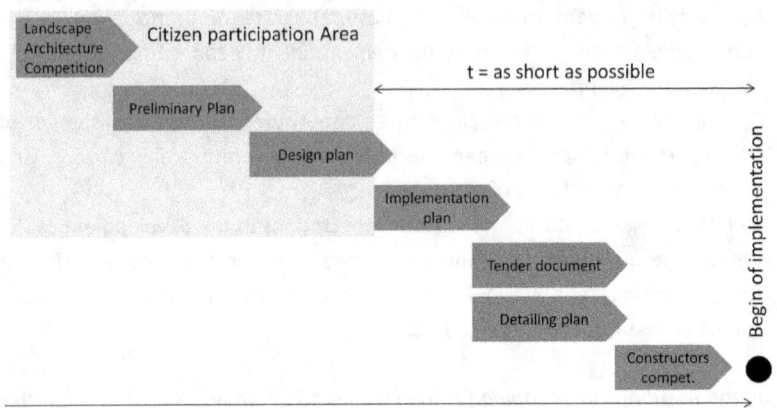

Figure 34: Planning time management and citizen participation

These parameters are the main challenges that the planners and coordination office have to deal with during the process. The complexity of managing a project requires experience; the citizens are not always aware of the constraints of the planning process. More information about planning mechanisms could improve the citizens' understanding regarding the complexity of urban development projects, and, therefore, minimize the potential frustration of citizens whose proposals are not integrated in the project due to technical restrictions.

In the case of *KTO* planning, the official participatory events began in December 2010. Without neglecting the planning parameters (contract issues, financial issues, etc.), it is possible to assume that participatory planning could have begun earlier, for example, right after the selection of the winning concept, in summer 2010. More time, therefore would have been allocated for the participatory events. The workshop for children and young people could have occurred in autumn. An additional citizen workshop to discuss the reviewed plans could have been included without compromising the next planning steps still ensuring sufficient time for the drafting of the design plans and the editing of the tender documentation (figure 35).

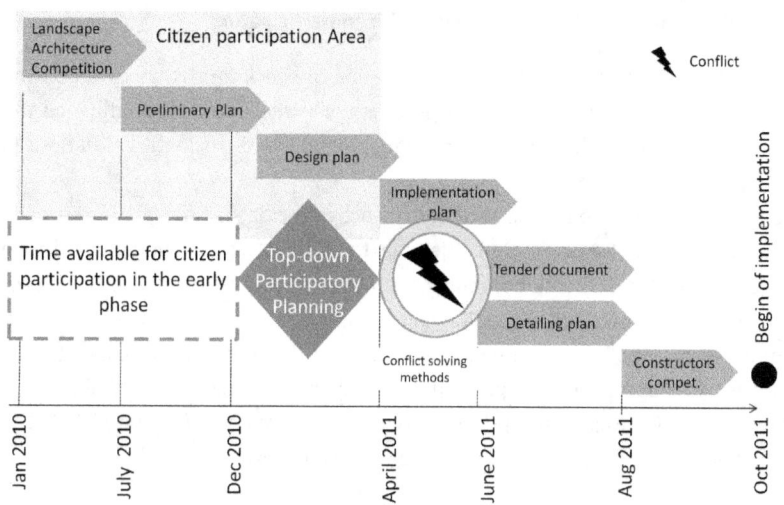

Figure 35: Potential improvement of the planning time management

7.3 Communication form for solving conflicts

As already suggested in the analysis of the fourth phase – a quest for consensus on the tree felling issue – a structured consensus finding process could have been more appropriate to solve the tree felling conflict. By organizing a round table with the planners, the citizens' initiatives and *AG Grün*, it could be assumed that an increase in the protests would have been minimized and that the political escalation initiated by citizen initiatives could have been avoided. The principles of the round table are that each group of divergent opinion is represented and has an equal right and duty in the discussion. The aim of the round table is to formulate proposals for the decision-makers, in this specific case to the Borough Administration (cf. chapter 4.3). In addition to minimizing the conflict step-up, an oriented consensus form could contribute to the following outcomes:

- Enhancement of the cohesion within civil society – *AG Grün* and citizens' initiatives – and therefore, strengthening their legitimacy
- Increase in trust between the public administration and civil society
- Awareness of the constraints in the projects and understanding of different opinions
- Increase in the autonomy of the institutional setting of *AZ* Program

7.4 Communication tools for an efficient citizen participation

The results of this analysis show the pertinence of the information paradox: the citizens' interest increases during the process while their power to influence the planning decreases (cf. chapter 1.3). This phenomenon leads to conflict situations in the late phases of the process.

The challenge of participatory planning is to activate citizens' interest in the early phases of planning. Several communication tools have been developed through practice (cf. chapter 4.3). The communication form should be attractive to citizens of Moabit with low social capital and suitable to the project's context. Communication about the planning, legal and formal constraints is a relevant basis for citizens to understand the participatory process. The 'linguistic' challenge of citizen participation identified in the theory can be overcome (cf. chapter 4.4). The following proposition has its real significance in this context:

> "Involve me and I shall understand." (Y. Iljine cited in Participation & Sustainable Development in Europe 2001)

The second aspect discovered through this analysis is that citizens' concerns should be identified and seriously taken into account in the process. Despite the fact that participatory planning took place between December 2010 and March 2011, the conflict on tree felling arose in April 2011. Nevertheless, this issue had been audible since spring 2010. By applying appropriate communication tools to solve this problem during the process, the conflict in the late phase could have been minimized. A partial conclusion of this analysis is that communication tools do not by themselves increase the efficiency of the participative planning, though a focused and flexible management of the participative process enables to increase the efficiency of the communication tools applied. This requires a precise understanding of the social context, and an ability to anticipate potential conflicts and to adapt the process according to the citizens' demands. Thus, collaboration between citizen leaders and experts to involve citizens and organize the process is crucial and beneficial for both sides – while citizen leaders can increase their legitimacy and their representativeness, the experts gain in efficiency and quality for the crafting of the planning.

8 Citizen within the local governance: The Stadtteilvertretung

In this chapter, the role of *StV* as community leader will be analyzed and the requirements for an efficient establishment of *StV* within the local governance are presented in a comparative analysis of both theory and practice. The following question will be answered: *"What are the prerequisites and limitations of citizens' involvement in the local governance?"*

8.1 Learning process towards consensus building

Regarding the form of *Beiratsrunde*, parallels with consensus building theory by Innes can be recognized (cf. Chapter 4.1). Thus, we can identify *StV* as a citizen representatives group, which is a partner within the local governance. *Beiratsrunde* established in the framework of *AZ* Program provides face-to-face discussion between the speakers of *StV* and the public administrations, represented by the Borough Administration and the Senate Administration; it is a communication space between the stakeholders. During *Beiratsrunde*, challenges are identified: potential conflicts emerging from different stakeholders' opinions, constraints of the outputs are recognized, issues which require an in-depth working process are named and responsibilities are shared between the different stakeholders (Hurny Nov 2011, Adner Nov 2011, Beiratsrunde Nov 2011).

As highlighted in Innes's definition of consensus building, "the process requires that participants have common information and that all become informed about each other's interests" (Innes 1996, p. 461). In *Beiratsrunde* of the *AZ* Program, the transparent exchange of information between the stakeholders is questionable. Indeed, *StV* members wish to be informed and involved in each others' actions and projects that occur in the framework of the *AZ* Program. KoSP does not consider that *StV* have to be involved in every project; *StV* is a 'participative tool' for the coordination of *AZ* Program, which is essential when projects require participation. Projects or actions taking place in the framework of *AZ* Program do not necessarily and automatically require citizen participation. In some cases, specific decisions are under the responsibilities of supra-ordinate authorities and beyond the responsibilities of the *AZ* institutional setting. Other projects are the responsibilities of the Borough Administration in the framework of *AZ* Program and can be categorized as 'traditional infrastructure maintenance', which does not require citizen participation (Beiratsrunde Nov 2011). Nevertheless, *StV* has to be informed about the activities that happen under the umbrella of *AZ* Program. This statement highlights the relevance of defining a clear sharing of responsibilities to avoid misunderstanding and frustration, which affect the efficiency of the collaborative work. This parameter corresponds with one of the conclusions of Gaventa's theory:

> "Develop and promulgate clear guidelines that clarify the appropriate 'rules and roles' for engagement between community leaders, government officials and the elected." (Gaventa 2004, p.32)

Another identified weakness of the *Beiratsrunde* with regard to a consensus building oriented process is the unequal distribution of powers between stakeholders. Gaventa identified the mutual recognition of the power relationships between the stakeholders as a requirement to enable an efficient integration of citizens in the local governance:

> "Name and address power relationships that surround participatory process, so that community leaders, local government officials and elected representatives participate on a 'level playing field' to the extent possible." (Gaventa 2004, p.32)

In reality, although *StV* is considered a partner in the process, the public authorities are the official decision-makers in the *AZ* Program and therefore can use their veto-power in *Beiratsrunde* as well as in the participatory process (figures 24, 27 and 29). However, public authorities fear losing their power, thus the establishment of citizen representative within the local governance is recognized in the theory as a threat. Nowadays, the collaboration between *StV* and the public administration is well established. Nevertheless, it was not the case in the early phases of the planning process of *KTO*: the lack of recognition of *AG Grün* as a partner contributed to a misunderstanding between the Borough Administration and *AG Grün* (cf. chapter 6.3). The positive evolution of the collaborative work during the last two years shows the potential and willingness of the public administrations to enhance the consensus-oriented communication form and consolidate trust-based relationships with *StV* speakers. The overall analysis of the collaborative work between *StV* and the public administration highlights the relevance of the stakeholders' open-mindedness and ability to self-criticize in taking advantage of a constructive learning process. This confirms that changes in participation forms require time and can only be achieved in a step-by-step process, and with the willingness of all partners to shift from their former behaviors towards a more open-mind interaction with the diverse stakeholders involved, as Gaventa (2004) previously stated.

8.2 Representativeness

Gaventa distinguishes two types of representativeness: (1) by the form of the representative's selection, and (2) by the skills of the representatives to fulfill the role of community leaders in local governance (cf. chapter 4.2).

Democratic and transparent election of the community representatives

Since the members of *StV* are elected by the population of Moabit for a two-year term, a democratic and transparent form of the selection of *StV* members is ensured. In theory, it would legitimate them to speak on behalf of the residents of Moabit. Nevertheless, the current members of *StV* have been elected by as little as a hundred voters. No data have been discovered in the course of this study regarding the social backgrounds of the voters. Nevertheless, by the testimony of the interviewed stakeholders, the tendency shows that most of the participants involved in the participatory process of *AZ* Program come from the privileged neighborhoods around the focus area, while the low-income citizens and the population with a migration history, who are living in the core of the focused area, are underrepresented in the participative process of *AZ* Program (Wilke Oct 2011). Since the high cultural diversity of Moabit is a relevant feature of the neighborhood (cf. chapter 5.2), the low rate of involvement of the population from diverse cultural backgrounds is a threat to the legitimacy of the elected members of *StV* to be considered representatives of the citizens. The analysis of the *StV* members' social and cultural backgrounds highlights the low 'statistical representativeness' of *StV* in terms of age structure, gender parity, level of professional background and migration history (Adner Nov 2011). Even if a 'formal' democratic and transparent election theoretically ensures the legitimacy of *StV* members, in practice the low rate of citizen participation – as individuals taking part in the participatory process – puts into perspective the low degree of representativeness and legitimacy of *StV* members to speak as citizen leaders. This reflects the soundness of Gaventa's statement which underlines that diverse forms of selection aim at being "democratic, transparent and relatively representative; often they are not" (Gaventa 2004, p.14).

Skills of StV members

The second definition of representativeness proposed by Gaventa focuses on the skills and abilities of citizen leaders to represent citizens within local governance.

The evaluation of the social capital of the members of *StV* is beyond the scope of this study. Nevertheless, some tentative conclusions can be drawn through observing and listening to the testimony of stakeholders. The goals of *StV* are clearly defined in the 'rules of procedure'. By agreeing to these goals, the members of *StV* are committed to do their utmost to reach them. The high degree of engagement that the members of *StV* show to work in as much a democratic process as possible allows for presuming a high degree of social capital between *StV* members. Their capacity to provide transparent documentation proves their high bureaucratic skills. This assumption is supported by Gaventa's theory concerning the high social capital of community representatives selected by a democratic election (cf. chapter 4.2). In this definition, the legitimacy of *StV* is ensured by the personal investment of its members for the citizens' common good. This assumption should be submitted to a further examination.

A low degree of legitimacy could affect the credibility of *StV*'s partnership with the public administrations or other organizations; additionally, it could threaten the guarantee of the integration of issues proposed by *StV*, which would contradict the public administrations' will. In the case of the *KTO* restructuring, the Borough Administration based its legitimacy on the *StV* resolution in which they agreed to support the plans for *KTO*. Nevertheless, the question of what would happen if *StV* did not support the plans of the Borough Administration is legitimate especially since the resolution to claim a moratorium on the tree felling, which was unanimously passed by the legally elected representative members of *BVV*, was rejected by the Borough Office. Therefore, the 'informal status' of *StV* appears as a threat to their influence in the case of contradictory opinions between the resolution voted by the *StV* and the expected objectives of the public administration. Based on this statement, it is possible to assume that the public authorities could easily overturn a *StV* decision. To ensure good partnership between the citizen representatives and the local government, Gaventa suggests to:

> "develop guidelines that help to clarify the different forms of accountability which underlie different forms of representation." (Gaventa 2004, p.32)

The official recognition of the *StV* speakers' group as a partner in the *Beiratsrunde* by the Borough Office (cf. chapter 5.4) shows the willingness of the public authorities to officially include citizens in the decision-making process; it can be interpreted as the first step towards the strengthening of "the legal or statutory provisions which enable participation" (Gaventa 2004, p.32), especially towards the legal provisions of citizen representatives within the local governance.

8.3 Stadtteilvertretung: 'outsiders-insiders' within the local governance?

StV – a well-established 'insider'

StV is a relevant partner of the Borough Administration since they are experts on the area, provide information and report the concerns of the citizens. Although the decisions they take during the *StV* monthly meeting are not legally binding, the Borough Administration considers their recommendations as relevant advice. According to the testimony of a *StV* speaker and of the public administration representatives, the work process in *Beiratsrunde* occurs in a constructive way and in a trusting atmosphere (Adner Nov 2011, Hurny Nov 2011). The established trust relationship between the stakeholders involved in *Beiratsrunde* confirms the integration of citizen representatives into the local governance.

StV – an unconvincing 'outsider'

Several observations lead to the conclusion that *StV* is deficient in its role as an 'outsider'. As developed in the first part of this chapter (*'Democratic and transparent election of the community representatives'*), *StV*'s low degree of legitimacy to represent citizens affected by *AZ* Program activities is the first critical indicator that *StV* fails to plays its role as an outsider. In addition to this argument, the dysfunction of *AG Grün* of *StV*, which was observed during the process, highlights the inability of *StV* to gather the citizens' opinions, to bring cohesion within civil society and to solve conflicting situations within the *StV* structure. Although the issue is rather complex, the dysfunction observed inside the structure of *StV* has to be taken into account to ensure the appropriate critical analysis. Indeed, the dissolution of *AG* is not an easy procedure and points out the necessity to question the efficacy of the workgroup in the *StV* working structure. Theory presented by Bischoff et al. (2005) emphasizes the relevance of defining the role of workgroups in the planning process (cf. chapter 4.3). By failing in its role as an outsider, *StV*, despite its intention, fed citizens' frustration and did not minimize the mistrust between citizens and the public authorities (figure 36).

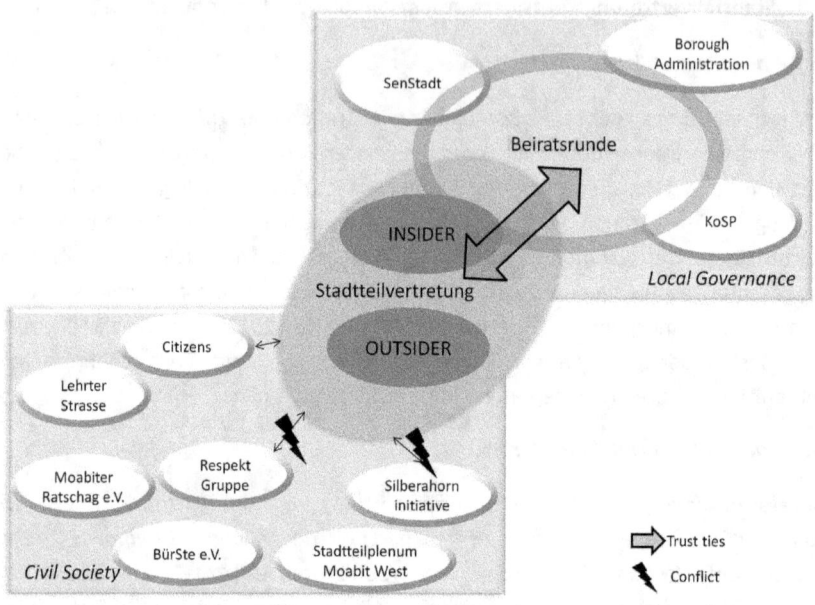

Figure 36: Current constellation of *StV* as outsider-insider

8.4 Identification of the allies of the Statdtteilvertretung

In order to strengthen its outsiders' role, *StV* should increase its legitimacy as a representative of the citizens of Moabit. Gaventa suggests using the existing community network and to identify allies within civil society and among politicians, who could support the tasks of the community leaders (Gaventa 2004).

Several citizen organizations are active in Moabit and have extensive experience in participation, such as BürSte e.V., Lehrter Straße e.V., and Moabiter Ratschlag e.V. These organizations have already established trust ties with the public administration. As a young actor within the landscape of citizens' entities in Moabit, *StV* has to take the opportunity to become integrated in the well-established structure and to create links with the larger and more diverse population of Moabit.

The myriad citizens' initiatives, founded to defend specific interests in the process of *AZ* Program, are composed of active citizens who gained experience in civil society mechanisms and have resources and energy to invest in the process of citizen participation. If the legitimacy and representativeness of the citizens initiatives are questionable, or can be identified as 'limited' according to the Gaventa's definitions, the large number of citizens that they manage to reach is not negligible in comparison to those that are reached by *StV*. Being aware that the issues promoted by *StV* and the issues defended by citizens' initiatives are different, the strategies applied by *StV* and the initiatives can be complementary. By combining their efforts, both citizens' entities can gain legitimacy. Moreover, the current emergence of *Piraten Partei* (Pirates Party) as a political representative on several level – from borough to city to federal levels – can be an opportunity for *StV*. Pirates Party supports new forms of direct and participative democracy, for instance through the development of eParticipation on the local as well as on the city level; and, it takes a stance for a stronger decentralization of decision-making on the borough level (Piraten Partei Deutschland Berlin 2011). Furthermore, the elected *BVV* is committed to the founding of a new committee called 'Transparency and Citizen Participation' (*Tranzparenz und Bürgerbeteiligung*) in the borough of Mitte (BVV Mitte 2011a). By identifying its 'allies' and strengthening its position in the existing network of civil society, *StV* would gain legitimacy among citizen organizations; it would increase its representativeness through dialog with groups with diverse opinions and, therefore, it would enhance its role of an 'outsider' in the local governance. A larger geographical establishment of *StV* in Moabit would also benefit the interests of the public administration by increasing its legitimacy and by building trust ties with civil society through *StV*. Between January 2009 and December 2011, *Leibniz-Institut für Regionalentwicklung und Stukturplanung* (IRS) conducted a research project called *'Urban pioneers in neighborhood – communication reconstruction of urban area in structural transformation'* (*'Raumpioniere im Stadtquartier - Zur kommunikativen (Re-) Konstruktion von Räumen im Strukturwandel'*), under the supervision of Gabriela Christmann. The task was to understand "how urban pioneers of a neighborhood can contribute to a communication process by their activities" (IRS 2009, p.5). The neighborhoods of Moabit and of Wilhelmsburg in Hamburg have been the field-research areas of the study. The outcomes of this research project could be used as a theoretical source to support the elaboration of sustainable development within the community of Moabit, and to identify the potential allies of *StV*.

8.5 Activating citizens to participate

To activate citizens as individuals to participate in the development of their neighborhood is a difficult task. As a coordinator of the participative process for *AZ*

Program projects, KoSP is highly involved alongside *StV* to promote the involvement of citizens. Since February 2011, the monthly newspaper *Ecke Turmstraße* has been published and distributed in highly frequented public spaces and stores of Moabit. The newspaper contributes to informing a large public about *AZ* Program. For instance, a presentation of the *KTO* restructuring planning was published in the first publication in February 2011 (Bezirksamt Mitte von Berlin 2011e), and in March 2011, a review of the planning workshop (February 12, 2011) was reported (Bezirksamt Mitte von Berlin 2011f). Two internet platforms are available: one is focused on *AZ Program*; it delivers updated information on the agenda of the program and documentation of recently held events (www.turmstraße.de). The second one is administrated by the members of *StV* and provides information on StV's work, activities and meeting agenda, as well as minutes from former meetings[12]. In addition to the periodical and continuous flow of information through the media mentioned above, a specific means of communication to inform and invite citizens to take part in the participatory events for the *KTO* restructuring project is based on flyer distribution and posters in public spaces or at the entrance of residential buildings around Moabit. A weekly meeting of *StV* (*Info-Stammtisch*) takes place in the Arminiushalle, in Moabit. These informal meetings aim to provide a space for discussion and exchange between the citizens of Moabit and the members of *StV*. *StV* tries to be present at every neighborhood festivity to promote their work and provide explanations about the institutional setting structure of *AZ Program*.

Despite the efforts to garner citizen participation in *AZ Program* activities, and contribute to the development of their neighborhood, the participants are few and do not represent the population of Moabit. In the minutes of the December 7, 2010 informative meeting, it is noted that a representative of *AG Grün* of *StV* "regretted the relatively low number of participants" (KoSP 2010, p.4). This statement is a common trend observed in the participatory process in general – one of the challenges of participation is to activate the citizens (Wilke Oct 2011). As stated in the 'rules of procedure' of *StV*, one of its four tasks is to activate and inform citizens about the projects of *AZ* Program. Several tools can be applied to outreach to citizens and involve them in the process (cf. chapter 4.3). Two of them will be presented here in more detail due to their high potential of adaptability in the context of Moabit: (i) eParticipation, and (ii) Forum. Although eParticipation is not a

---

[12] For further information: www.stv-turmstraße.de

Results of the analysis

direct efficient tool to activate citizen participation, it increases the transfer of information and exchange of citizens' opinions (cf. chapter 4.3). *StV*'s Internet platform provides a space for presenting information and sharing concerns regarding their activities and resolutions. While the *StV* forum is not commonly used by citizens, the Internet platform MoabitOnline is a well-established and known platform for the exchange of information and opinions regarding neighborhood development in Moabit (cf. chapter 5.3). By collaborating with the administrators of MoabitOnline, *StV* could take advantage of the platform to collect citizens' concerns and inform them about *AZ* Program activities, which would contribute to the collection of concerns from a larger part of the population. It would also contribute to the identification of divergent opinions of Moabit citizens, who are not necessarily represented by the 27 members of *StV*. This would help to avoid potential conflict situations. As previously mentioned, Pirates Party, identified as potential 'allies' for *StV*, could bring political support to the development of eParticipation on the local level as a new instrument, which would be complementary to the face-to-face discussions between citizens and the public administration. The established and well-visited forum of Moabit West (cf. chapter 5.3*)* promotes the idea that a regularly organized forum for *AZ* Program could be an efficient communication tool.

8.6 Support for capacity building development

The outcomes of the analysis point out an array of opportunities that *StV* could explore to strengthen its representativeness, legitimacy and, therefore, its empowerment on the local level. On the other hand, the efficiency of *StV* as 'insider-outsider' partner required high bureaucratic abilities and a high degree of social capital. These are real challenges for the members of *StV*, who have different interests by being involved in the *StV*. Capacity building requires time and financial support. *StV* would benefit from the retrospective assessment of their activities and actions, which can be internally conducted by the members of *StV*. Additionally, external support from experts in participation processes would provide meaningful inputs to support the enhancement of the working organization of *StV*. If *StV* seeks to become a partner in local urban governance and expects to be seen as such it requires professionalism and constant analysis and self-evaluation of its on-going working process. This would be beneficial to assess the current Strengths and Weaknesses which guided the previous activities of *StV* and to identify Opportunities and Threats for the further development of the group's working structure. This analysis corresponds to the so-called SWOT Analysis. To apply such an accurate analytical methodology, support from external experts appears to be required.

8.7 Prerequisites and limitations of citizens' involvement in local governance

Before answering the question, it is relevant to point out that being a partner within the local governance implies that *StV* is an insider and an outsider at the same time. This is the challenge and the complexity of citizen representatives within local governance. *Beiratsrunde* is a promising space for consensus building. Nevertheless, clear and legally binding rules are necessary in order to define which level of involvement is required for each of the issues discussed. The positive evaluation of the process over the last two years means that one can expect a further legal formalization of *StV*'s involvement in the future. Regarding the role as outsiders, their low representativeness is a real threat for the legitimacy of *StV*, and, therefore, a threat for its empowerment within the local governance. By taking advantage of the existing active citizens' organization networks and by collaborating with KoSP in the organization of the 'top-down' participative process, *StV* could strengthen its legitimacy and become a coordinator of civil society in the mid-term (figure 37).

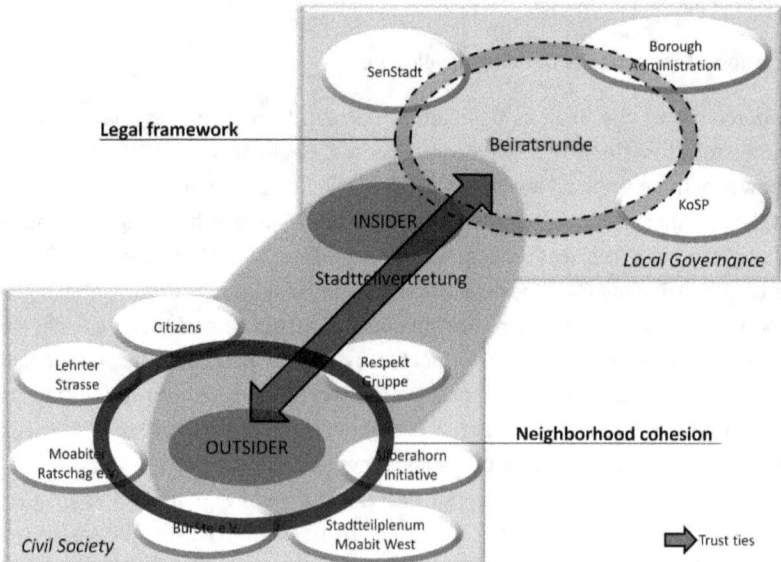

Figure 37: Ideal constellation of *StV* as outsider-insider

9 Results of the analysis

The goal of analyzing the planning process of the *KTO* restructuring, set forth in the beginning of the study, has been to identify the role of citizens in the institutional setting of the urban renewal program *AZ Turmstraße*, and to verify if citizen involvement in this case study contributes to strengthening the trust between the public administration of Berlin and the civil society in the neighborhood of Moabit. The theory and empirical analysis herein presented show that citizens can play two roles: (i) as individual citizens serving as field-experts that are partaking in the mixed 'top-down' participatory planning of the program, and (ii) as citizen representatives within the local urban governance working towards consensus building.

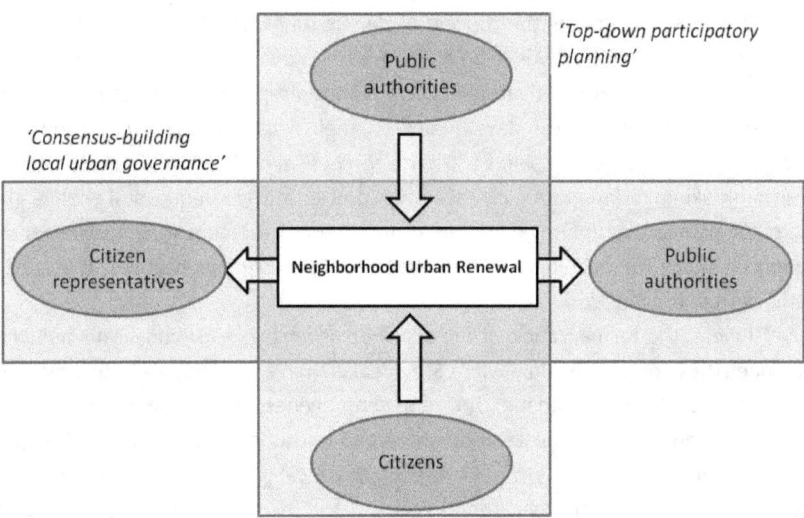

Figure 38: 'Top-down' participatory planning and consensus building in *AZ* Program

In theory, urban scholars agree unanimously that citizen participation contributes to strengthening the trust between public authorities and civil society. An appropriate form of collaboration to build a trusting relationship is the establishment of consensus building. *Beiratsrunde* is the key tool in the institutional setting of *AZ Program*, which is identified in the analysis as the forum of communication between the partners. The analysis shows that the current organization of *Beiratsrunde* has a solid basis to ensure decision-making through a common deliberative process tending towards consensus finding. Nevertheless, the key principles identified in the theory of the consensus finding process that ensures an efficient collaborative planning are not anchored in the current institutional setting of AZ Program and would need enhancement in two ways: (i) power is still unequally distributed between the partners, and (ii) communication and information sharing is not transparent enough between the partners and for the rest of civil society. As suggested by the theoretical recommendations derived from the academic debate, a committed and legally binding code defining the responsibilities of each stakeholder group and the interaction rules between them should contribute to reinforcing the structural basis of *Beiratsrunde* as a consensus building form for decision-making for AZ Program. Two empirical observations provide the rationale for the application of innovative tools for sharing the process of decision-making: (i) the current political willingness of the Senate to develop a new form of governance, which includes the citizens, and (ii) the high motivation of current citizen representatives to invest their time, energy and skills in the development of their neighborhood. Such innovative local governance structures will contribute to confirming the legitimacy of shared decision-making, to integrating civil society representatives as equal stakeholders in the planning and decision-making process and, therefore, to ensuring a sustainable, beneficial space for building new ties between citizen representatives and public authorities in the long run.

Nevertheless, the formalization of *Beiratsrunde* as an arena for consensus building will meet these objectives only when *StV* speakers have the legitimacy to speak on behalf of the citizens of Moabit. The representativeness of *StV* members is a sine qua none condition for the establishment of the institutional setting of AZ Program as a sustainable and efficient structure of the local governance. The abundant literature on the citizen representativeness issue highlights the importance of identifying a local context oriented definition of citizen leader representativeness. While the current structure of *StV* aims to meet as close as possible a representative democratic form to develop proposals and vote on resolutions, the analysis of this case highlights structural dysfunctions and weaknesses in the role of *StV* members as representatives of citizens' interests. The members of *StV* should design an efficient communication strategy to reach two of their commonly defined objectives:

> "The elected StV for the AZ Program and renewal urban area Turmstraße participates in the planning and re-vitalization of the center of Moabit and ensures that the competenc-

es, the knowledge and the needs of the residents of Moabit are taken into account in the planning. [...] The StV aims by its work to involve actively the citizens and to inform citizens about the ongoing projects and actions." (Stadtteilvertretung Turmstraße 2011, p.1)

The use of the existing network of diverse, innovative and well-established active citizen entities in Moabit, as well as the 'top-down' participative process run by the coordination office KoSP, provide opportunities for *StV* members to reach citizens with diverse migration histories, social backgrounds and different degrees of social capital. By identifying groups with divergent opinion within civil society and encouraging discussion between these groups, *StV* could play the role of a coordinator of civil society and take advantage of the citizens' investment and efforts towards consensus building within civil society, which would help strengthen the community's cohesion.

By recognizing *StV* as a potential and promising future community leader within the local governance, the study supports a concept that citizens possess the abilities to strengthen the ties between civil society and public authorities towards a local deliberative democracy. This will contribute to give more independence to the local urban governance and therefore will avoid political interference between the borough level and the neighborhood level, such as the ones observed during the planning process of *KTO*. Gaventa summarized brilliantly this idea as follows:

"Neighbourhood regeneration and democratic renewal go hand-in-hand" (Gaventa 2004, p.32).

10 Conclusion

The current tendency in urban governance policies towards collaborative planning promotes citizens involvement within the local urban governance. This orientation is the result of a long evolution of urban politics, which led to the shift from 'government' to 'governance' and has its roots in the middle of the 20th century. This trend has been observed around the world with international urban policies supporting citizen participation.

In Berlin, the citizens' willingness to be involved in urban politics has led to a current situation in which politicians and public authorities are recognizing that civil society should be involved in planning and decision-making. The guidelines developed by the Berlin Senate orient the principles of urban policies towards neighborhood renewal with citizens as key stakeholders in the process. This corresponds to the international and European directives for urban policy setting in the beginning of the 21st century.

In practice, the growing gap between civil society and public authorities, as well as the citizens' frustration regarding decision-making, begs the question of the efficiency of the forms of participation currently in practice. Participation takes place in two forms, which are complementary: (i) citizens involvement as field-experts in 'top-down' participatory planning steered by public authorities (decision-makers and veto-players) and urban experts (process coordinators), and (ii) involvement of citizen representatives within local governance, as partners of the public authorities with the objective of reaching deliberative decisions (through consensus building). The scope of urban renewal programs allows these two types of participation to be applied; by encouraging communication in planning, these programs support a 'top-down' participatory process and by including citizens in the institutional setting, these programs promote collaborative planning in local governance. In the framework of this study, such programs appear to be a privileged space for developing innovative forms of participation. The development of ties based on trust between public authorities and civil society can be strengthened and will contribute to the establishment of long-term citizen involvement in urban local governance. Citizens involvement in the institutional setting of urban renewal programs can be seen as a 'starting point' towards the establishment of citizen representatives in local governance, and therefore in the decision-making process for neighborhood development.

'Top-down' participatory planning requires high expertise regarding social context and the availability of resources to effectively put communicative tools to use. Activating citizens in the early phases of the process is one of the greatest challenges. The adaptability of the communication tools to the target group's profile, the flexibility of the process to react to potential conflict situations, and the legal formalization of the participatory processes' results would ensure a more efficient 'top-down' participatory planning – the main aspects underlying this study. The consensus-oriented partnership between citizen representatives and public authorities is based in theory on equal power sharing and on the ability of the citizen representatives to fulfill their defined role under the 'outsiders-insiders' concept. High degrees of social capital, negotiation skills and important time investment are required to fulfill this highly complex double function, which highlights the limitations of the applicability of this concept in practice. This partnership is often threatened by the low representativeness and legitimacy of citizen representatives. However, public authorities also play a double function in this constellation: as a veto-player in the 'top-down' participatory planning, and as a partner in the consensus building. In practice, the fear of losing their decision-making power limits the establishment of a true equal power and therefore undermines a stable decision-making process such as consensus building.

The analytical results of this study establish that the two forms of participation are strongly interdependent. The legitimacy of the citizen representatives is based on their ability to collect the diverse citizens' opinions and to encourage the strengthening of community cohesion. This can only be achieved through an intensive and continuous effort to activate citizens and, therefore, 'top-down' participatory planning is a crucial support. It would increase the legitimacy of the representative citizens in the framework of urban renewal programs. This statement highlights the limitation of citizen participation in a long-term process. Hence, it begs the question to be addressed in further research on sustainability of local citizen participation beyond urban renewal programs. In Moabit, the involvement of citizen representatives within the local governance is currently ensured through the framework of the urban renewal program *Aktives Stadtzentrum*. The lack of a legally-binding commitment from the side of administration threatens the role of *Stadtteilvertretung* as a partner in the local governance in the long-term. On the other hand, a long-term establishment of citizens in local governance challenges the current form of representative democracy. This leads to a second potential study, which could focus on complementarities and discrepancies between the role of citizen within the local governance and the role of legally elected representatives. It will be interesting to investigate to what extent participative democracy and representative democracy can be complementary.

Empirical evidence proved that the society has the ability to overcome the current challenges of participation. However, consolidation of collaborative planning on the local level is fundamentally dependent on the willingness of citizens and public authorities to strengthen community cohesion and to make choices for a common good.

11 Appendixes

Appendix 1 - Communication forms

Based on
Bischoff et al 2005, pp.317-322

		Suitability for work in target group		Amount of participants		Suitability according to the planning phases			Intensity of citizens' involvement		Schedule		Interest representation		Legal frame		Setting	
		not appropriate	appropriate	limited	large	Implementation	Planning	Target definition	involved	informed	long-term	time limited	indirect	direct	informal	formal	several tools	unique tool
	To gather information																	
	Written questionnaire	x	x			x	x	x		x		x	x	x				x
	Interview	x	x			x	x		x			x	x	x				x
	Activating Survey	x	x			x	x	x	x			x		x	x			x
	Complaint Management	x			x	x	x	x	x	x		x		x	x			x
	E-Information		x		x	x	x	x		x	x		x			x		x
INFORM	**To inform and build opinion**																	
	Announcement of projects		x			x	x	x	x			x	x		x			x
	Exhibition		x		x	x	x			x		x	x		x			x
	Local press		x		x	x		x		x		x	x		x			x
	Campaign		x		x	x	x		x		x	x	x		x		x	
	Citizens meeting	x			x	x	x	x	x			x		x		x		x
	Citizens question time	x			x	x	x	x		x		x		x		x		x
	Presentation and discussion		x		x	x	x	x		x		x		x	x			x
	Field trip		x	x		x	x	x		x		x		x	x			x
	Site meeting		x	x		x	x	x	x			x		x	x			x
	Public disclosure	x			x		x		x	x		x		x		x		x
	Hearing and discussion	x			x		x		x	x		x		x		x		x
	Petition and citizens' request	x			x		x	x	x			x	x		x			x
	Ombudsman		x		x	x	x	x	x		x		x			x		x
	Council and committee		x	x		x	x	x	x		x			x		x		x
	Referendum	x			x		x	x	x			x		x		x		x
	Citizen oriented consultation		x		x	x	x	x	x	x		x		x	x			x
PARTICIPATE	Local ideas action		x	x		x	x	x	x			x		x	x		x	
	Workgroup		x	x		x	x	x	x			x		x	x			x
	Citizen jury	x			x		x	x	x			x		x	x		x	
	Planning for Real		x		x	x	x	x	x	x		x		x	x		x	
	Future oriented workshop		x	x			x	x	x			x		x	x		x	
	Action Planning	x			x		x	x	x			x		x	x		x	
	Future Search Conference	x			x		x	x	x			x		x	x		x	
	Real Time Strategic Change	x			x		x	x	x	x		x		x	x		x	
	Community Organizing		x		x	x	x	x	x		x		x		x	x		x
	Participatory Rapid Appraisal		x	x			x	x	x			x		x	x		x	
	Target groups participation		x	x			x	x	x		x		x		x	x		x
	E-Participation	x			x	x	x	x		x		x		x		x		x
	Advocacy planner		x	x		x	x	x			x		x	x	x		x	
	Workshop		x	x		x	x	x			x		x	x	x			x
COOPERATE	Forum		x	x		x	x	x	x			x	x		x	x		x
	Round Table		x	x		x	x	x			x		x	x	x			x
	Mediation	x			x	x	x	x			x		x	x	x			x
	Open Space		x	x			x		x			x		x	x			x
	Intermediate organization		x	x		x	x	x		x	x		x	x	x			
	local partnership		x	x		x	x	x		x	x		x	x	x			

Appendix 2 - Rules of Procedure Stadtteilvertretung *Turmstraße*
im Aktiven Zentrum und Sanierungsgebiet Turmstraße

STADTTEIL
VERTRETUNG
TURMSTRASSE

Geschäftsordnung

(Von der Stadtteilvertretung beschlossen am 11. und 25.07.2011)

Übersicht

	Präambel	Seite 1
§ 1	Zusammensetzung	Seite 1
§ 2	Sitzungen	Seite 2
§ 3	Protokollführung	Seite 2
§ 4	Geschäftsführung	Seite 2
§ 5	Arbeitsgruppen (AGs)	Seite 3
§ 6	Öffentlichkeitsarbeit	Seite 4
§ 7	Finanzen	Seite 4
§ 8	Beschlussfassung	Seite 5
§ 9	Inkrafttreten	Seite 5

Präambel

(1) Die gewählte Stadtteilvertretung für das Bund-Länder-Förderprogramm „Aktives Zentrum Turmstraße" und das „Sanierungsgebiet Turmstraße" beteiligt sich an der Planung und Umgestaltung des Moabiter Zentrums, um dafür zu sorgen, dass die Kompetenz, das Wissen und die Bedürfnisse der MoabiterInnen bei den Planungen berücksichtigt werden.

(2) Die Stadtteilvertretung hat das Ziel, im freundschaftlichen Miteinander einen wesentlichen und ideenreichen Beitrag zur Verbesserung der Attraktivität und Aufenthaltsqualität des Gebietes Turmstraße zu leisten.

(3) Der Stadtteilvertretung ist es wichtig, dass die ökonomische Balance eines angebotsreichen Versorgungszentrums wieder hergestellt und dabei dem Reichtum kultureller und kreativer Vielfalt, die den Charakter und das Flair der Moabiter Insel prägen, Rechnung getragen wird.

(4) Die Stadtteilvertretung hat bei ihrer Arbeit das Ziel, die BürgerInnen aktiv einzubeziehen und über vorliegende Planungen und Aktivitäten zu informieren.

§ 1 Zusammensetzung

(1) Die Stadtteilvertretung setzt sich aus den auf einer Stadtteilversammlung gewählten Mitgliedern zusammen, die für 2 Jahre gewählt werden.

(2) Wahlbereich ist die Moabiter Insel.
Wahlberechtigt und wählbar sind alle Personen,
- die mindestens 16 Jahre alt sind
und im Wahlbereich
- mit ihrem Wohnsitz polizeilich gemeldet sind oder
- als EigentümerIn, WohnungseigentümerIn, Erbbauberechtigte oder PächterIn Rechte an einem Grundstück haben oder
- als Gewerbetreibende oder freiberuflich Tätige ihren Betrieb oder ihre

Stadtteilvertretung Turmstraße • Geschäftsordnung 2011 • Seite 2

Praxis haben oder
- als ArbeitnehmerIn ihren / seinen Arbeitsplatz in einem Betrieb oder einer Praxis haben oder
- gesellschaftlich oder ehrenamtlich für Moabit tätig sind.

Nach dreimalig aufeinander folgender, unentschuldigter Abwesenheit an Regelsitzungen der Stadtteilvertretung, die aus den jeweiligen Protokollen hervorgehen muss, wird den betreffenden Mitgliedern die Beendigung ihrer Mitgliedschaft nahe gelegt.

(4) Vorgezogene Neuwahlen sind erforderlich, wenn
- sich die Stadtteilvertretung mit Zweidrittel-Mehrheit der anwesenden Mitglieder aufgelöst,
- mehr als die Hälfte der StadtteilvertreterInnen die Beendigung ihrer Mitarbeit in der Stadtteilvertretung erklärt hat oder
- die Stadtteilvertretung in drei aufeinander folgenden Regelsitzungen gemäß § 8 (1) beschlussunfähig war.

§ 2 Sitzungen

(1) Die SprecherInnen laden zu den Sitzungen der Stadtteilvertretung, die grundsätzlich öffentlich sind, ein. Die Öffentlichkeit kann auf Antrag aus begründetem Anlass ausgeschlossen werden.

(2) Die Stadtteilvertretung tritt in der Regel monatlich zu einer Sitzung zusammen.

(3) Ein Viertel der Mitglieder kann eine außerordentliche Sitzung verlangen.

§ 3 Protokollführung

(1) Jede Sitzung der Stadtteilvertretung wird in einem Ergebnisprotokoll festgehalten. Der Protokoll-Entwurf wird den SprecherInnen spätestens zwei Wochen nach der Sitzung zur Verfügung gestellt.

(2) Das von den SprecherInnen autorisierte Protokoll wird den Mitgliedern in der Regel spätestens eine Woche vor der nächsten Sitzung zur Verfügung gestellt.

(3) Das Protokoll einer Sitzung wird jeweils zu Beginn der nächsten Sitzung verabschiedet, ist damit frei gegeben und wird der Öffentlichkeit zugänglich gemacht.

§ 4 Geschäftsführung

(1) - Die Stadtteilvertretung wählt aus ihrer Mitte fünf gleichberechtigte SprecherInnen sowie weitere fünf StellvertreterInnen, die die Stadtteilvertretung vertreten. Sie werden jeweils für ein Jahr gewählt.
- Nach dreimalig aufeinander folgender unentschuldigter Abwesenheit an Regelsitzungen der Stadtteilvertretung und / oder Beiratssitzungen, die aus den jeweiligen Protokollen hervorgehen muss, verliert das Mitglied seine Funktion als SprecherIn.

Stadtteilvertretung Turmstraße • Geschäftsordnung 2011 • Seite 3

(2) Die Funktion der SprecherInnen als auch der StellvertreterInnen sollte zu gleichen Teilen von Frauen und Männern besetzt werden und sollte die unterschiedlichen AGs repräsentieren.

(3) Die SprecherInnen werden mit einfacher Mehrheit gewählt. Sie können auf Antrag mit Zweidrittel-Mehrheit bei Anwesenheit von mehr als der Hälfte der Mitglieder abgewählt werden.

(4) Aufgaben der SprecherInnen sind:
- die Vertretung der Stadtteilvertretung im Beirat: Die SprecherInnen vertreten die Stadtteilvertretung und ihre Positionen bei den Beiratssitzungen von Verwaltung und deren Beauftragten und berichten dem Plenum regelmäßig darüber. Wenn ein/e SprecherIn zu einer Beiratssitzung nicht erscheinen kann, sorgt sie bzw. er für eine Stellvertretung,
- im Plenum: Sitzungsvorbereitung und Einladung, Sitzungsleitung, Sicherstellen der Protokolle.
- Vertretung der Stadtteilvertretung nach außen.
- Weiterleitung von Informationen und Terminen an die Mitglieder der Stadtteilvertretung.

Die SprecherInnen können Aufgaben an Mitglieder der Stadtteilvertretung delegieren.

(5) Die SprecherInnen informieren die Stadtteilvertretung regelmäßig über ihre Tätigkeiten.

(6) Die SprecherInnen erstellen in Zusammenarbeit mit den KoordinatorInnen der Arbeitsgruppen und dem / der KassenwartIn jährlich einen Finanzplan. Der Finanzplan wird von der Stadtteilvertretung beschlossen.

§ 5 Arbeitsgruppen (AGs)

(1) Die Stadtteilvertretung bildet offene AGs zu verschiedenen Schwerpunktthemen.

(2) Die AGs sind Gremien der Stadtteilvertretung und können sich sowohl mit langfristigen Planungen als auch mit kurzfristig aktuellen, zeitlich begrenzten Projekten befassen.

(3) Leitung der AGs:
- Für jede AG der Stadtteilvertretung gibt es eine/n KoordinatorIn. Die KoordinatorInnen müssen Mitglieder der Stadtteilvertretung sein und werden von allen Mitgliedern der AG gewählt.
- Die KoordinatorInnen
  - gewährleisten, dass die Beschlüsse und Anregungen der Stadtteilvertretung in den AGs vermittelt und umgesetzt werden,
  - berichten regelmäßig im Plenum der Stadtteilvertretung über die Ergebnisse der AGs,
  - bringen Beschlussvorlagen der AGs ins Plenum ein und
  - organisieren die Einladungen zu den Sitzungen der AGs.

Stadtteilvertretung Turmstraße • Geschäftsordnung 2011 • Seite 4

(4) Aufgaben der AGs:
- Die AGs erarbeiten für die Stadtteilvertretung entscheidungsreife Vorlagen.
- Sie berichten während der Sitzungen der Stadtteilvertretung von ihrer Arbeit und erhalten dafür ausreichend Zeit für eine Erörterung der Themen im Plenum.

(5) Kompetenzen der AGs:
- Die AGs sind an die Beschlüsse der Stadtteilvertretung gebunden. Sie sind nicht autonom.
- Stellungnahmen der AGs nach außen erfolgen ausschließlich durch die SprecherInnen der Stadtteilvertretung, die AG Öffentlichkeitsarbeit oder die KoordinatorInnen der AGs.
- Im Namen einer AG dürfen keine Positionen nach außen getragen werden, die den Beschlüssen der Stadtteilvertretung in Wortlaut oder Sinn widersprechen.

§ 6 Öffentlichkeitsarbeit

(1) Die Öffentlichkeitsarbeit ist ein wesentlicher Bestandteil der Arbeit der Stadtteilvertretung. Sie beinhaltet,
- auf vielfältige Weise Informationen über Beschlüsse der Stadtteilvertretung und andere wichtige Informationen aus dem Aktionsbereich der Stadtteilvertretung zu verbreiten und
- den BürgerInnen die Prozesse transparent zu machen, damit sie sich aktiv einbringen können,
- in Bezirks- und Senatsverwaltung hinein zu wirken und Prozesse zu vermitteln sowie für die Ergebnisse zu werben.

(2) Beschlüsse der Stadtteilvertretung werden gemeinsam nach außen als solche vertreten. Minderheitenpositionen sind zu berücksichtigen und erkennbar zu machen.

(3) Veröffentlichungen der Stadtteilvertretung erfolgen durch die SprecherInnen.
Schriftliche Erklärungen sind inhaltlich von zwei SprecherInnen oder deren Stellvertretungen zu autorisieren.
Schriftliche Erklärungen sind den Mitgliedern der Stadtteilvertretung unverzüglich, spätestens aber auf der nächsten Sitzung vorzulegen.

(4) Die SprecherInnen können Aufgaben im Bereich der Öffentlichkeitsarbeit an die AG Öffentlichkeitsarbeit und / oder bei sachlichem Bezug an eine/n KoordinatorIn einer AG delegieren.

§ 7 Finanzen

(1) Die Stadtteilvertretung beschließt den Jahresfinanzplan für das Kalenderjahr. Die Stadtteilvertretung verfügt in Abstimmung mit dem Bezirksamt über die von diesem bereit gestellten Gelder.

(2) Die Stadtteilvertretung wählt aus ihrer Mitte eine/n KassenwartIn und zwei RechnungsprüferInnen.

Stadtteilvertretung Turmstraße • Geschäftsordnung 2011 • Seite 5

(3) Für die Stadtteilvertretung wird ein Konto eingerichtet. Zeichnungsberechtigt ist der / die KassenwartIn gemeinsam mit einem / einer SprecherIn.

(4) Der / die KassenwartIn ist der Stadtteilvertretung gegenüber rechenschaftspflichtig. Nach Abschluss des Kalenderjahres ist von dem / der KassenwartIn ein Kassenbericht vorzulegen, der von den RechnungsprüferInnen geprüft wird. Die Entlastung des Kassenwarts / des Kassenwartin erfolgt durch die Stadtteilvertretung.

(5) Über die Verwendung der Finanzmittel beschließt die Stadtteilvertretung mit einfacher Mehrheit.

§ 8 Beschlussfassung

(1) Die Stadtteilvertretung ist beschlussfähig, wenn mindestens die Hälfte der StadtteilvertreterInnen anwesend ist.

(2) Beschlüsse werden mit einfacher Mehrheit der anwesenden Mitglieder der Stadtteilvertretung gefasst.

(3) Bei Beschlussunfähigkeit ist die Stadtteilvertretung bezüglich der entsprechenden Beschlussanträge in nächstfolgender Sitzung unabhängig von der Anzahl der anwesenden Mitglieder beschlussfähig, soweit unter Mitteilung der Tagesordnung und mit Hinweis auf die besondere Beschlussfähigkeit eine Woche vorher in Textform zu der Sitzung eingeladen wurde.
Bei dreimaliger aufeinander folgender Beschlussunfähigkeit wird nach § 1 (4) verfahren.

(4) Bei Beschlussfassung werden Minderheitenvoten im Protokoll festgehalten.

(5) Änderungen der Geschäftsordnung bedürfen einer Zweidrittel-Mehrheit der anwesenden Mitglieder der Stadtteilvertretung.

(6) Mitglieder der Stadtteilvertretung dürfen an Beschlüssen nicht mitwirken, wenn sie an dem zur Abstimmung stehenden Thema wirtschaftlich Beteiligte sind oder von wirtschaftlich Beteiligten Entgelte erhalten.

(7) Bei Zweifeln über den Ausschluss bei der Beschlussfassung wegen persönlicher Beteiligung entscheidet die Stadtteilvertretung in der entsprechenden Sitzung ohne Stimmrecht des Betroffenen.

§ 9 Inkrafttreten

(1) Die Geschäftsordnung tritt durch Beschluss von mindestens zwei Dritteln der anwesenden Mitglieder der Stadtteilvertretung in Kraft.

(2) Die Geschäftsordnung tritt mit dem 25.7.2011 in Kraft.
Sie bleibt über die Wahl einer neuen Stadtteilvertretung hinaus bis zu ihrer Bestätigung oder Neufassung in Kraft.

12 Table of figures

Cover	Latz+Partner Landscape Architecture Concept for the regeneration of the park Kleiner Tiergarten / Ottopark, Berlin. © Latz + Partner 2012.	
Figure 1	**Information Paradox** By the author based on Reinert, A. (1996)'Bürgergutachten ÜSTRA zum ÖPNV in Hannover', in Selle, K. (ed.), Planung und Kommunikation - Gestaltung von Planungsprozessen in Quartier, Stadt und Landschaft - Grundlagen, Methoden, Praxiserfahrungen, Berlin: Bauverlag, p. 326-328.	9
Figure 2	**Framework and dimensions of sustainable urban development** Deutscher Städtetag (2011) Integrierte Stadtentwicklungsplanung und Stadtentwicklungsmanagement – Strategien und Instrumente nachhaltiger Stadtentwicklung, Position paper approved by Präsidium des Deutschen Städtetages on its 383rd session, 22 Mar, Hannover. (Translated by the author)	17
Figure 3	**Urban Renewal Programs in Berlin** Based on a photograph taken by the author at the exhibition Aktive Zentren, Senatsverwaltung für Stadtentwicklung Berlin, Aug 2011, designed by Isabelle Delatte.	20
Figure 4	**Field-work based on snow-ball principle** By the author.	22
Figure 5	**Chronological process of the field research from August to December 2011** By the author.	23
Figure 6	**Parallels between the stakeholders analysis (left) and the methodological process applied in this study (right)** By the author based on Reed et al (2009, p. 1947).	25
Figure 7	**The social Capital Continuum** Uphoff, N. (1999) 'Understanding social capital: Learning from the analysis and experience of participation', in Serageldin, I., ed., Social Capital: A multifaceted perspective, Washington, DC: World Bank, 215-253.	30
Figure 8	**Level of involvement** By the author based on SenStadt (2011) Handbuch Partizipation, Berlin: Kulturbuch-Verlag GmbH, p.28.	31
Figure 9	**Community representatives as 'insiders-outsiders'** By the author.	33

Figure 10	Aktive Zentren in Berlin SenStadt ([undated]) Förderprogram Aktive Stadtzentren [online], available: http://www.stadtentwicklung.berlin.de/staedtebau/foerderprogramme/aktive_zentren/de/gebiete/index.shtml [accessed: 30/11/2011].	44
Figure 11	Moabit, neighborhood of the borough Berlin-Mitte Designed by Isabelle Delatte based on SenStadtUm (2012) Karte Bezirke Berlin, held by Herr Welsch, SenStadtUm.	45
Figure 12	Streets map in the surroundings of *KTO* By the author, designed by Isabelle Delatte based on © Google Maps 2012: Moabit, available: http://maps.google.fr/ [accessed: 30/08/2012].	46
Figure 13	Urban poles of attraction in the surounding of Moabit By the author, designed by Isabelle Delatte based on © Google Maps 2012: Moabit, available: http://maps.google.fr/ [accessed: 30/08/2012].	46
Figure 14	Development Index Berlin 2010 Designed by Isabelle Delatte based on SenStadtUm (2012a) Development Index Berlin 2010, held by Stutenbecker, SenStadtUm Berlin.	47
Figure 15	Urban renewal programs in Mitte SenStadtUm (2012b) Aktionsraum plus Wedding/Moabit , held by Karen, SenStadtUm Berlin.	49
Figure 16	Aktives Stadtzentrum and Turmstraße 'renewal urban area' KoSP (2011) 'Aktives Stadtzentrum und Sanierungsgebiet Turmstraße', 1:6000.	49
Figure 17	Neighborhood participation in Moabit Bezirksamt Mitte von Berlin (2011) Quartiersbeteiligungen, 1:10000.	51
Figure 18	MoabitOnline 'Space' for different communicative actions IRS (2011) Figure designed by Leibniz-Institut für Regionalentwicklung und Strukturplanung (IRS) (www.irs-net.de), Forschungsabteilung 3 „Kommunikations- und Wissensdynamiken im Raum"; central figure: MoabitOnline, held by Christmann.	53
Figure 19	Structure of the *AZ* Program from the federal to the neighborhood level By the author.	57
Figure 20	Overview map of the two KTO planning sections © Latz + Partner 2012	59

Tables of figures

Figure 21	Overview map of the seven KTO implementation sections © Latz + Partner 2012.	59
Figure 22	Latz+Partner Landscape Architecture Concept © Latz + Partner 2012.	60
Figure 23	Main events of the planning process By the author	62
Figure 24	Categories of stakeholders involved in the first phase By the author	64
Figure 25	Podium discussion on December 7, 2010 KoSP (2011) Dokumentation der Planungswerkstatt am 12. Februar 2011 zur Umgestaltung des Ottoplatzes, des Ottoparks und des westlichen Kleinen Tiergartens [online], available: http://www.turmstraße.de/downloads/pdf/oeffentlichkeitsarbeit/buergerbeteiligung/110419_KTO_Doku_Planungswerkstatt.pdf [accessed: 31/11/2011].	68
Figure 26	Moabiter Ratschlag e.V. Flyer Moabiter Ratschlag e.V. (2011) Jugendbeteiligungsprojekt Umgestaltugn Ottopark und Spielplatz Zwinglistraße [online], available: http://www.turmstraße.de/downloads/pdf/oeffentlichkeitsarbeit/buergerbeteiligung/120308_KTO_Doku_Jugendbeteiligung_Ottopark.pdf [accessed: 30/11/2012].	69
Figure 27	Categories of stakeholders involved in the third phase By the author.	71
Figure 28	Citizens' Workshop on February 12, 2011 KoSP (2011) Dokumentation der Planungswerkstatt am 12. Februar 2011 zur Umgestaltung des Ottoplatzes, des Ottoparks und des westlichen Kleinen Tiergartens [online], available: http://www.turmstraße.de/downloads/pdf/oeffentlichkeitsarbeit/buergerbeteiligung/110419_KTO_Doku_Planungswerkstatt.pdf [accessed: 31/11/2011].	73
Figure 29	Categories of stakeholders involved in the fourth phase By the author.	75
Figure 30	Interpretation of the consensus building process by the stakeholders By the author based on Hartnett, T. ([undated])'The Basis of Consensus Decision Making' [online], available: http://www.groupfacilitation.net/Articles%20for%20Facilitators/The%20Basics%20of%20Consensus%20Decision%20Making.html [accessed: 30/11/2011].	76

Figure 31	Information board for the KTO restructuring tagged by tree protector activists By the author (17/11/2011).	80
Figure 32	Citizens channels to reach the decision-making sphere in KTO restructuring planning By the author.	82
Figure 33	Citizens' involvement in key-steps of the planning process and areas for improvement By the author.	84
Figure 34	Planning time management and citizen participation By the author.	86
Figure 35	Potential improvement of the planning time management By the author.	87
Figure 36	Current constellation of the StV as outsider-insider StV By the author.	94
Figure 37	Ideal constellation of StV as outsider-insider By the author.	98
Figure 38	'Top-down' participatory planning and consensus building in AZ Program By the author.	99

13 References

PUBLICATIONS

Abgeordnetenhaus Berlin (2006) *Lokale Agenda 21 - Berlin zukunftsfähig gestalten Lokale Agenda 21*, Berlin: Abgeordnetenhaus Berlin.

Amt für Statistik Berlin Brandenburg (2011) Statistischer Bericht, A I 5 -hj 1/11, Potsdam: Amt für Statistik Berlin Brandenburg.

Arnstein, S. (1969) 'A Ladder of Citizen Participation', JAIP, Vol. 35, No. 4, 216-224.

Barnes, M., Skelcher, C., Beirens, H., Dalziel, R., Jefarres, S. and Wilson, L. (2008) *Designing citizen-centred governance*, York: Joseph Rowntree Foundation.

Barnes, M., Sullivan, H., Knops, A. and Newman, J.(2004) 'Power, Participation and Political Renewal: Issues from a Study of Public Participation in Two English Cities', *IDS Bulletin*, Volume 35, Issue 2, 58-66.

Bezirksamt Mitte von Berlin (2011a) 'Das ist Baumquälerei', Ecke Turmstraße, October - November 2011, 2-3.

Bezirksamt Mitte von Berlin (2011e) 'Die kleiner Tiergarten soll heller werden', Ecke Turmstraße, February 2011, 4.

Bezirksamt Mitte von Berlin (2011f) 'Belegung erwünscht', Ecke Turmstraße, March 2011, 4.

Bezirksamt Mitte von Berlin, Latz + Partner and KoSP (2010) Kleiner Tiergarten / Ottopark - Information zur Umgestaltung, Berlin: Bezirksamt Mitte von Berlin, Latz + Partner and KoSP.

Bischoff, A., Selle, K. and Sinning, H. (2005) Informieren, Beteiligen, Kooperieren: Kommunikation in Planungsprozessen; eine Übersicht zu Formen, Verfahren und Methoden, Dortmund: Dortmunder Vertrieb für Bau- und Planungsliteratur.

BMVBS (2011) Aktive Stadt- und Ortsteilzentren - drei Jahre Praxis, Berlin: Bundesinstitut für Bau-, Stadt- und Raumforschung.

BMVBS and BBR (2007) Auf dem Weg zur einer nationalen Stadtentwicklungspolitik, FaDCM: Meckelheim.

Bodenschatz, H. (1987) Platz frei für das Neue Berlin!, Berlin: Institut für Stadt- und Regionalplanung der TU Berlin.

Bodenschatz, H. (2010) Berlin Urban Design - A Brief History, Berlin: DOM publishers.

Bodenschatz, H., Ernst, K. and Polívka, J. (2007) Revitalisierung innerstädtischer Stadtteilzentren: Ein Schlüssel zur Renaissance der Innenstadt - Beitrag zu einer notwendigen Debate, held by Technische Universität Berlin, Fakultät VI, Institut für Soziologie.

Chaskin, R.-J. and Abunimah, A. (1997) 'A View from the City: Local Government Perspectives on Neighbourhood-based Governance in Community-Building Initiatives', Discussion Paper, Chicago: Chapin Hall Centre for Children, University of Chicago.

Commission of the European Communities (2001) European Governance, A White Paper, COM (2001) 428, Brussels: Commission of the European Communities.

Denscombe (2007) The Good Research Guide for small-scale social research projects, 3d ed., New-York: Open UP Study Skills.

Die Landesabstimmungsleiterin (2011) Direkte Demokratie in Berlin, Berlin: Die Landesabstimmungsleiterin.

Dienel, Peter C. (1978) Die Planungszelle - Eine Alternative zur Establishment-Demokratie - Der Bürger plant seine Umwelt, Braunschweig: Opladen.

Döhler, M. (2007) 'Hierarchie', in Benz, A., Lütz, S., Schimank, U. and Simonis, G., eds., Handbuch Governance, Theoretische Grundlagen und empirische Anwendungsfelder, Wiesbaden: VS Verlag für Sozialwissenschaften, 46-53.

Drilling, M. and Schnur, O. (2009) *Governance der Quartiersentwicklung*, Wiesbaden: VS Verlag für Sozialwissenschaften.

Fassbinder, H. (1997) Stadtforum Berlin - Einübung in kooperative Planung, Dortmund: Dortmunder Vertr. für Bau- und Planungsliteratur.

Fenster, E. (2001) 'Bürgerbeteiligung bei der Stadtentwicklung - das Beispiel Berlin-Moabit', in Regiestelle E&C der Stiftung SPI (ed.), Zweite Regionalkonferenz der Region Ost, Berlin: Regiestelle E&C der Stiftung SPI.

Foot, J. (2009) Citizen involvement in local governance, York: Joseph Rowntree Foundation.

Forrest, R. and Kearns, A. (2001) 'Social Cohesion, Social Capital and the Neighbourhood', *Urban studies*, Vol. 38, No. 12, 2125-2143.

References

Gibson, P. D., Lacy, D. L. and Dougherty, M. J. (2005) 'Improving Performance and Accountability in Local Government with Citizen Participation', The Innovation Journal: The Public Sector Innovation Journal Volume 10(1).

Girling, C., Kellett, R. and Johnstone, S. (2006) 'Informing Design Charettes: Tools for participation in neighbourhood-scale planning', The Integrated Assessment Journal, Vol. 6, Iss. 4, 109-130.

Gittell, M., Newman, K., Bockmeyer, J., Lindsay, R. (1998) 'Expanding Civic Opportunity: Urban Empowerment Zones', Urban Affairs Review, 33:4, 530-558.

Hamedinger, A. (2010) 'Partizipation in der Raumentwicklung - eine Frage von "politischer Kultur" und "Good Governance"?', in Zech, S., *Partizipativ planen - Raum entwickeln*, Berlin: LIT Verlag, 23-35.

Häussermann, H., Läpple, D. and Siebel, W. (2008) Stadtpolitik, Frankfurt am Main: Suhrkamp Verlag.

Healey, P. (1997) Collaborative Planning - Shaping places in fragmented societies, London: Macmillan Press Ltd.

Hilpert, J. (2011) 'Nutzen und Risiken öffentlicher Großprojekte: Bürgerbeteiligung als Voraussetzung für eine größere gesellschaftliche Akzeptanz', *Stuttgarter Beiträge zur Risiko- und Nachhaltigkeitsforschung*, Nr. 19.

Holtkamp, L. (2007) 'Local Governance', in Benz, A., Lütz, S., Schimank, U. and Simonis, G., eds., Handbuch Governance, Theoretische Grundlagen und empirische Anwendungsfelder, Wiesbaden: VS Verlag für Sozialwissenschaften, 366-377.

Hüttinger, H. and Selle, K. (2008) 'Bürgerorientierung in Not?', vhw, 3 (2008), 160-166.

Innes, J. (1996) 'Planning Through Consensus Building: A New View of the Comprehensive Planning Ideal', *Journal of the American Planning Association*, 62(4), 460-472.

Innes, J. E., and Booher, D. E. (2004) 'Reframing Public Participation: Strategies for the 21st Century', *Planning Theory & Practice,* Vol. 5, No. 4, 419–436.

IRS (2009) 'Raumpioniere im Stadtquartier: Zur kommunikativen (Re-) Konstruktion von Räumen im Strukturwandel, IRS: Erkner.

Jakubowski, P. (2007) 'Urban Governance: Stimmt die Balance zwischen Legitimation und Effizienz?', Städte im Umbruch, Volume 4/2007, 22-28.

Johnson, H. and Wilson, G. (2000) 'Biting the bullet: Civil society, social learning and the transformation of local governance', World Development, 28 (11), 1891-1906.

Kubicek, H. (2010) 'The potential of E-Participation in Urban Planning: A European Perspective', in Carlos S. N., ed, *Handbook of research of E-Planning: ICTs for Urban Development and Monitoring*, Hershey: Information Science Reference, 168-194.

Kubicek, H., Lippa, B. and Koop, Alexander (2011) Erfolgreich beteiligt? Nutzen und Erfolgsfaktoren internetgestützter Bürgerbeteiligung - Eine empirische Analyse von 12 Fallbeispielen, Gütersloh: Verlag Bertelsmann Stiftung.

Ley, A. and Weitz, L. (2003) 'Praxis Bürgerbeteiligung – Ein Methodenhandbuch', *Arbeitshilfe Nr. 30, Agenda Transfer*, Bonn: Agentur für Nachhaltigkeit und Stiftung Mitarbeit.

Lübke, I. (2010) 'Kooperationen in der Stadtentwicklung - Eine Einführung', in Lübke, I., ed., *Kooperative Stadtentwicklung durch kooperative Planung*, Dietrich Reimer Verlag GmbH: Berlin, 8-16.

Metropolis (2011) *Integrated Urban Development - The way forward*, Barcelona: Metropolis World.

Power, A. (2004) 'Neighborhood Management and the Future of Urban Areas', CASEpaper 77, Centre for Analysis of Social Exclusion, London: London School of Economics.

Reed, M., Graves, A., Dandy, N., Posthumus, H., Hubacek, K., Morris, J., Prell, C., Quinne, C. and Stringer, L. (2009) 'Who's in and why? A typology of stakeholder analysis methods for natural resource management', Journal of environmental management, 90, 1933-1949.

Selle, K. (1996) Planung und Kommunikation - Gestaltung von Planungsprozessen in Quartier, Stadt und Landschaft - Grundlagen, Methoden, Praxiserfahrungen, Berlin: Bauverlag.

SenStadt (2009) Handbuch zur Sozialraumorientierung Grundlage der integrierten Stadt(teil)entwicklung Berlin, Berlin: Senatverwaltung für Stadtentwicklung.

SenStadt (2010b) Integriertes Stadtteilentwicklungskonzept Aktionsraum plus Wedding/Moabit, Berlin: S.T.E.R.N..

SenStadt (2011) Handbuch Partizipation, Berlin: Kulturbuch-Verlag GmbH.

SenStadt (2011a) Stadtforum Berlin: Füße - Fahrrad - Auto - Wer bekommt wie viel vom Straßenraum? - Dokumentation der Veranstaltung am 24. Februar 2011, Berlin: Senatsverwaltung für Stadtentwicklung.

Siebel, W. (2010) 'Planende Verwaltung und zivile Gesellschaft', in Becker, E. et al., eds., *Stadtentwicklung, Zivilgesellschaft und bürgerschaftliches Engagement*, Stuttgart: Lucius & Lucius Verlagsgesellschaft mbH, 25-38.

UN-Habitat (2001) Building Bridges between citizens and local governments through participatory planning, UN-Habitat.

Uphoff, N. (1999) 'Understanding social capital: Learning from the analysis and experience of participation', in Serageldin, I., ed., *Social Capital: A multifaceted perspective*, Washington, DC: World Bank, 215-253.

VvB (2010) Verfassung von Berlin, Berlin: Abgeordnetenhaus von Berlin.

INTERNET SOURCES

AG Grün (2010) Anregung für die Auslobung des landschaftsplanerischen Wettbewerbs KTO - Kleiner Tiergarten/Ottopark [online], available: http://www.stadtteilvertretung-turmstraße.de/gr%C3%BCn/anregungen-auslobung-landschaf [accessed: 30/11/2011].

Antz, E.-M. (2006) 'Wie lässt sich das freiwillige Engagement für Nachhaltigkeit stärken', speech 23-25th Oct, Postdam, available: http://www.forum-nachhaltige-regionen.net/download_de/Antz_23.10.06_de.pdf [accessed 30/11/2011].

Baumann, F. (2002) Erfolgsbedingungen kooperativer Stadtentwicklung, Erfahrungen aus dem Berliner Agenda 21 Prozess, Kooperative Planung und Mediation im Konfliktfall [online], available: http://www.bueroblau.de/pdf/Erfolgsbedingungen.pdf [accessed 30 July 2011].

Beratungsgesellschaft für Stadterneuerung und Modernisierung mbH ([undated]) Geschichte - Grundsätze der behutsamen Stadterneuerung [online], available: http://www.sanierung-berlin.de/sanberlin/Geschichte/geschichte.html [accessed: 30/11/2011].

Berliner Zeitung (2011) 'Proteste - Polizei schützt Baumfällung im Ottopark' [online], available: http://www.bz-berlin.de/bezirk/tiergarten/polizei-schuetzt-baumfaellung-am-ottopark-article1288167.html [accessed: 14/12/2011].

Bezirksamt Mitte von Berlin (2010) Drucksache 1725/III, 09/11/2010 [online], available: http://www.berlin.de/ba-mitte/bvv-online/vo020.asp?VOLFDNR=4118& options=4 [accessed: 30/11/2011].

Bezirksamt Mitte von Berlin (2011) Drucksache Nr. 1937 III, 03/06/2011 [online], available: http://www.berlin.de/ba-mitte/bvv-online/vo020.asp?VOLFDNR=4330 &options=4 [accessed: 30/11/2011].

Bezirksamt Mitte von Berlin (2011b) Beschluss Drucksache 2223/III 04/11/2011 - Mediationsverfahren zur Beachtung von Einwänden bei der Umgestaltung von Ottopark und Kleinem Tiergarten (westlicher Teil) durchführen!, 04/11/2011, [online], availbale: http://www.berlin.de/ba-mitte/bvv-online/vo020.asp?VOLFDNR=4616 &options=4 [accessed: 30/11/2011].

Bezirksamt Mitte von Berlin (2011c) Beschlusstext der Vermerk von Bau AL vom 21.09.2011 Drucksache Nr. 2223 III [online], available: http://www.berlin.de/ba-mitte/bvv-online/___tmp/tmp/45081036252887301/252887301/00082465/65-Anlagen/07/Drs_2223_Mediation_KTO_Anlage.pdf [accessed 30/11/2011].

Bezirksamt Mitte von Berlin (2011d) Drucksachen 2223/III, 06/12/2011, [online], available: http://www.berlin.de/ba-mitte/bvv-online/vo020.asp?VOLFDNR=4616 &options=4 [accessed: 12/12/2011].

Bezirksamt Mitte von Berlin, BSM and BUE ([undated]) 'Kurzfassung - Aktives Stadtzentrum Turmstraße' online, available: http://www.stadtentwicklung.berlin.de /staedtebau/foerderprogramme/aktive_stadtzentren/download/wettbewerbsbeitrag_turmstraße.pdf [accessed:30/11/2011].

Bodenschatz, H. and Polinna, C. (2010) Learning from IBA - die IBA 1987 in Berlin, Paper prepared for Senatsverwaltung für Stadtentwicklung [unpublished].

Borstel, S. (von) (2010) 'Kommunen greifen Bund und Länder an', *DIE WELT*, 16 Feb, available: http://www.welt.de/die-welt/politik/article6414678/Kommunen-greifen-Bund-und-Laender-an.html [accessed: 12/01/2012].

Brandt, W. (1969) 'Daring More Democracy (October 28 1969)' in Jarausch, K. H. and Welsh; H. A., eds., Two Germanies (1961-1989), available: http://germahistorydocs.ghi-dc.org/sub_document.cfm?document_id=901 [accessed: 10/01/2012].

BUND and NABU (2011) Offener Brief, to Fraktion die Linke Bezirksvertreterversammlung Berlin-Mitte [online], available: http://www.moabitonline.de/wp-content/uploads/2011/04/anschreibenBVVMitte_Verb%C3%A4nde_07102011.pdf [accessed 07/11/2011].

References

BVV Mitte (2011) Beschluss - Drucksache 2223/III, 16/09/2011 [online], available: http://www.berlin.de/ba-mitte/bvv-online/vo020.asp?VOLFDNR=4616&options=4 [accessed: 30/11/2011].

BVV Mitte (2011a) Drucksache 0006/IV, 18/11/2011 [online], available: http://www.berlin.de/ba-mitte/bvv-online/vo020.asp?VOLFDNR=4642&options=4 [accessed: 12/01/2012].

Charter of European Cities & Towns Towards Sustainability (1994) Aalborg, Denmark on 27 May [online], available: http://sustainable-cities.eu/upload/pdf_files/ac_english.pdf [accessed: 18/11/2011].

Fiedler, J. (2011) Streit um Bäume in Moabit - Licht gegen Schatten im Moabit, 29/09/2011 [online], available: http://taz.de/Streit-um-Baeume-in-Moabit/!79035/ [accessed: 30/11/2011].

Firouzi, Y, Robert, A.-D., Nake, R. and Nake-Mann, B. (2011) 'Soziale Nähe der Bäume im Kleinen Tiergarten / Ottopark' [online], available: http://www.moabiton line.de/wp-content/uploads/2011/04/Appell_110423.pdf [accessed: 30/11/2011].

Gaventa, J. (2004) Representation, Community Leadership and Participation: Citizen Involvement in Neighbourhood Renewal and Local Governance. Paper prepared for the Neighbourhood Renewal Unit Office of the Deputy Prime Minister, Institute of Development Studies [unpublished].

Jacobs, S. and Heine, H. (2011) 'Parkstreit in Berlin - Im Ottopark sollen Bäume fallen', Tagesspiegel, 28/09/2011 [online] available: http://www.tagesspiegel.de/berlin/parkstreit-in-berlin-im-ottopark-sollen-baeume-fallen/4666018.html [accessed: 30/11/2011].

KoSP (2010) Protokoll Bürgerversammlung zur Umgestaltung des Kleinen Tiergartens/Ottoparks [online], available: http://www.turmstraße.de/downloads/pdf/oe ffentlichkeitsarbeit/buergerbeteiligung/110415_KTO_Protokoll_Veranstaltung.pdf [accessed: 30/11/2011].

KoSP (2011) Dokumentation der Planungswerkstatt am 12. Februar 2011 zur Umgestaltung des Ottoplatzes, des Ottoparks und des westlichen Kleinen Tiergartens [online], available: http://www.turmstraße.de/downloads/pdf/oeffentlichkeits arbeit/buergerbeteiligung/110419_KTO_Doku_Planungswerkstatt.pdf [accessed: 31/11/2011].

Landwehrkanal-blog (2011) 'Massenfällung im Ottopark' [online], available: http://baumschutz.wordpress.com/2011/10/04/ottoparkfaellungen/#more-14659 [accessed: 12/12/2011].

Leipzig Charta (2007) Leipzig Charta zur nachhaltigen europäischen Stadt, 24. Mai [online], available: http://www.eu2007.de/de/News/download_docs/Mai/0524-AN/075DokumentLeipzigCharta.pdf, [accessed: 30/09/2011].

Moabiter Ratschlag e.V. (2011) Jugendbeteiligungsprojekt Umgestaltung Ottopark und Spielplatz Zwinglistraße [online], available: http://www.turmstraße.de/downloads/pdf/oeffentlichkeitsarbeit/buergerbeteiligung/120308_KTO_Doku_Jugendbeteiligung_Ottopark.pdf [accessed: 30/11/2012].

MoabitOnline ([undated]) 'Beiträge zum Stichwort 'Gentrifizierung" [online], available: http://www.moabitonline.de/tag/gentrifizierung [accessed: 30/11/2011].

MoabitOnline (2010) 'Einladung auf die Wiese im Kleinen Tiergarten', Moabitonline [online], available: http://www.moabitonline.de/3916 [accessed 05/11/2011].

MoabitOnline (2011) 'Welche Bäume sollen gefällt werden und warum?' [online], available: http://www.moabitonline.de/8110 [accessed: 30/11/2011].

NABU Landesverband Berlin (2011) 'Baumschutz trifft auf Ignoranz' [online], available: http://berlin.nabu.de/themen/baumschutz/baumschutz-news/14221.html [accessed: 14/12/2011].

Nationale Stadtentwicklungspolitik (2008) 'Bürger für ihre Stadt aktivieren' [online], available: http://www.nationale-stadtentwicklungspolitik.de/cln_032/nn_251602/Content/Artikel/schwerpunktthemen.html#target3 [accessed: 30/11/2011].

OECD (2005) Strengthening Trust in Government: What Role for Government in the 21st Century?, Conclusions of a Meeting of the Public Governance Committee at Ministerial Level [online], available: http://www.oecd.org/dataoecd/35/22/41958688.pdf [accessed: 30/11/2011].

Participation & Sustainable Development in Europe (2001) Methods [online], available: http://www.partizipation.at/methods.html [accessed: 30/11/2011].

Partizipation und nachhaltige Entwicklung in Europa (undated) Praxiswissen [online], available: http://www.partizipation.at/praxiswissen.html [accessed: 30/11/2011].

Piraten Partei Deutschland Berlin (2011) Grundsatzprogramm Wahl 2011 [online], available: http://www.piratenpartei.de/politik/wahl-und-grundsatzprogramme/ [accessed:30/11/2012].

PSS [undated] Zukunftsinitiative Stadtteil [online], available: http://www.pss-berlin.eu/content/e3781/index_ger.html, [30/09/2011].

Quartiersmanagement Moabit Ost (2010) 'Präsentation der Entwürfe' [online], available: http://www.moabit-ost.de/Umgestaltung-kl-Tiergarten-Ottopark.575. 98.html [accessed 07/11/2011].

Sager, T. (2002) 'Deliberative Planning and Decision Making - An Impossibility Result', Journal of Planning Education and Research, Sage, online, available: http://jpe.sagepub.com/content/21/4/367, [accessed: 30/11/2011].

Selle, K. (2011) 'Something went wrong - Oder: Vom langen Weg zur Lokalen Beteiligungskultur', pnd online, II/2011, available: http://www.planung-neu-denken.de/content/view/201/46 [30/11/2011].

SenStadt ([undated]) Förderprogram Aktive Stadtzentren [online], available: http://www.stadtentwicklung.berlin.de/staedtebau/foerderprogramme/aktive_zen tren/de/gebiete/index.shtml [accessed: 30/11/2011].

SenStadt ([undated-a]) Aktionsräume Plus - Ziele [online], available: http://www.stadtentwicklung.berlin.de/soziale_stadt/aktionsraeume_plus/de/ziele .shtml [accessed: 10/01/2012].

SenStadt (2009a) Entwicklungsindex Soziale Stadtentwicklung 2010 auf Ebene der Planungsräume (LOR), [online], available: http://www.stadtentwicklung.berlin.de/planen/basisdaten_stadtentwicklung/monitoring/de/2010/karten.shtml [accessed: 30/11/2011].

SenStadt (2010) Kleiner Tiergarten/Ottopark Berlin Mitte Nichtoffener landschaftspanerischer Realisierungswettbewerb Ergebnisprotokoll [online], available: http://www.turmstraße.de/downloads/pdf/projekte/kleiner-tiergarten/110415_W ettbewerb_Ergebnisprotokoll.pdf [accessed: 30/11/2011].

SenStadt (2010a) Kleiner Tiergarten / Ottopark Berlin-Mitte Nichtoffener landschaftsplanerischer Realisierungswettbewerb Auslobung [online], available: http://www.ak-berlin.de/publicity/ak/internet.nsf/0/C33070E2D23FF57FC12578F F004AADD5/$FILE/auslobung%20Ottopark.pdf [accessed: 30/11/2011].

SenStadt (2011b) Förmliche Festlegung neuer Sanierungsgebiete, Senatsbeschluss vom 15. März 2011, Pressestelle, available: http://www.aktion-kms.de/files/1103 15_senat_handout_sanierungsgebiete_2011.pdf [accessed: 30/11/2011].

SenStadt (2011c) Stadtentwicklungsplan Verkehr [online], available: http://stadtentwicklung.berlin.de/verkehr/politik_planung/step_verkehr/downloa d/Stadtentwicklungsplan_Verkehr_Berlin_ohne_Anhaenge.pdf [accessed: 13/01/2012].

Silberahorn and other citizens (2011) 'Appell - Umdenken bevor Kettensägen und Bagger in den Kleinen Tiergarten und Ottopark kommen!' [online], available: http://www.moabitonline.de/wp-content/uploads/2011/04/Appell_110423.pdf [accessed: 30/11/2011].

SPD Alt Moabit (2011) 'Spallek verweigert Bürgerbeteiligung' [online], available: http://www.spd-altmoabit.de/2011/12/spallek-verweigert-burgerbeteiligung/ [accessed: 12/01/2012].

Stadtteilvertretung Turmstraße (2011) Geschäftsordnung Stadtteilvertretung Turmstraße, 11-25/07/2011 [in Appendix of this study].

Stadtteilvertretung Turmstraße (2011a) Stellungnahme der StV Turmstraße zur Umgestaltung des Kleinen Tiergartens/Ottoparks [online], available: http://www.stadtteilvertretung-turmstraße.de/stadtteilvertretung/stellungnahme-stv-turmstraße [accessed: 30/11/2011].

Torka, S. (2010) 'B-Laden, der kleine Nachbarschaftsladen in der Lehrter Straße' [online], available: http://www.bmgev.de/mieterecho/archiv/2010/detailansicht/ article/b-laden-der-kleine-nachbarschaftsladen-in-der-lehrter-straße.html [accessed: 01/12/2011].

UNDP (1997) *Good governance and sustainable human development*, policy document [online], available: http://www.pogar.org/publications/other/undp/gover nance/undppolicydoc97-e.pdf [30/09/2011].

United Nations (1992) United Nations Conference on Environment & Development - Agenda 21, available: http://www.un.org/esa/sustdev/documents/agenda21/ english/Agenda21.pdf [accessed: 30/11/2011].

United Nations Public Administration Programme (2005) Toward Participatory and Transparent Governance [online], available: http://www.unpan.org/DPADM/ Events/GlobalForum/6thGlobalForum/tabid/602/language/en-US/Default.aspx [accessed: 30/11/2011].

Velasquez, M., Andre, C., Shanks, T., S. J. and Meyer, M. J. (1992) 'The Common Good' [online], *Issues in Ethics*,V5, N1 (Spring 1992) available: http://www.scu.edu/ethics/practicing/decision/commongood.html [accessed: 12/01/2012].

Wegweiser Bürgergesellschaft (undated) 'Praxishilfe' [online], http://www.buergergesellschaft.de/praxishilfen/103674/ [accessed: 30/11/2011].

OTHER SOURCES (Interviews, meeting reports, private documentations)

Adner, A. (Nov 2011) Interview 14.11.2011, by the author.

AG Grün (2009) 'Kleiner Tiergarten/Ottopark im Programm Aktives Stadtzentrum Turmstraße', letter to Constanze Hurny, 12 Dec, held by Nake-Mann [unpublished].

Amannsberger, K. (Dec 2011) Interview 08.12.2011, by the author.

Beiratsrunde (Nov 2011) Report of the 19th Beiratsrunde, 09.11.2011, by the author.

complan Kommunalberatung (2011) Programmleitfaden Aktive Zentren Berlin, held by Frau Hurny [unpublished].

Gruber, G. and Stegmeier, M. (Dec 2011) Correspondence, by the author.

Homann, K. (Nov 2011) Interview 17.11.2011, by the author.

Hurny, C. (Nov 2011) Interview 08.11.2011, by the author.

IRS (2011) Figure designed by Leibniz-Institut für Regionalentwicklung und Strukturplanung (IRS) (www.irs-net.de), Forschungsabteilung 3 "Kommunikations- und Wissensdynamiken im Raum"; central figure: MoabitOnline, held by Christmann.

Nake-Mann, B. (2010) Informationsveranstaltung der StV Turmstraße, 29.6.2010, held by Nake-Mann [unpublished].

Nake-Mann, B. (Dec 2011) Interview 02.12.2011, by the author.

Nake-Mann, B. (Dec 2011a) Correspondence, by the author.

SenStadt (2008) 'Programm "Aktive Stadtzentren"', letter to Vorsitzenden des Hauptausschusses.

Silberahorn (2011) Letter to the fractions of the borough assembly Mitte, 02/09/2011, held by Nake-Mann.

Stadtteilvertretung Turmstraße (2011b) Beschluss-Anträge für das Plenum der StV T am 24.10.2011, held by Adner [unpublished].

Verwaltungsgericht Berlin (2011) Beschluss, VG 24 L 338.11, held by Hurny.

Wilke, A. (Oct 2011) Interview 14.10.2011, by the author.

Sie haben die Wahl:
Bestellen Sie die Schriftenreihe
Städtebau – Architektur – Gesellschaft
einzeln oder im **Abonnement**

per E-Mail: vertrieb@ibidem-verlag.de | per Fax (0511/262 2201)
als Brief (*ibidem*-Verlag | Leuschnerstr. 40 | 30457 Hannover)

Bestellformular

☐ Ich abonniere die Schriftenreihe *Städtebau – Architektur – Gesellschaft* ab Band # ____

☐ Ich bestelle die folgenden Bände der Schriftenreihe *Städtebau – Architektur – Gesellschaft*

____; ____; ____; ____; ____; ____; ____; ____; ____

Lieferanschrift:

Vorname, Name ....

Anschrift ....

E-Mail.. | Tel.: ....

Datum .... | Unterschrift ....

Ihre Abonnement-Vorteile im Überblick:
- Sie erhalten jedes Buch der Schriftenreihe pünktlich zum Erscheinungstermin – immer aktuell, ohne weitere Bestellung durch Sie.
- Das Abonnement ist jederzeit kündbar.
- Die Lieferung ist innerhalb Deutschlands versandkostenfrei.
- Bei Nichtgefallen können Sie jedes Buch innerhalb von 14 Tagen an uns zurücksenden.

ibidem-Verlag

Melchiorstr. 15

D-70439 Stuttgart

info@ibidem-verlag.de

www.ibidem-verlag.de
www.ibidem.eu
www.edition-noema.de
www.autorenbetreuung.de

www.ingramcontent.com/pod-product-compliance
Lightning Source LLC
Chambersburg PA
CBHW051813230426
43672CB00012B/2723